Van Bibber and

Richard Harding Davis

Alpha Editions

This edition published in 2024

ISBN : 9789362926845

Design and Setting By
Alpha Editions
www.alphaedis.com
Email - info@alphaedis.com

Contents

HER FIRST APPEARANCE

It was at the end of the first act of the first night of "The Sultana," and every member of the Lester Comic Opera Company, from Lester himself down to the wardrobe woman's son, who would have had to work if his mother lost her place, was sick with anxiety.

There is perhaps only one other place as feverish as it is behind the scenes on the first night of a comic opera, and that is a newspaper office on the last night of a Presidential campaign, when the returns are being flashed on the canvas outside, and the mob is howling, and the editor-in-chief is expecting to go to the Court of St. James if the election comes his way, and the office-boy is betting his wages that it won't.

Such nights as these try men's souls; but Van Bibber passed the stage-door man with as calmly polite a nod as though the piece had been running a hundred nights, and the manager was thinking up souvenirs for the one hundred and fiftieth, and the prima donna had, as usual, began to hint for a new set of costumes. The stage-door keeper hesitated and was lost, and Van Bibber stepped into the unsuppressed excitement of the place with a pleased sniff at the familiar smell of paint and burning gas, and the dusty odor that came from the scene-lofts above.

For a moment he hesitated in the cross-lights and confusion about him, failing to recognize in their new costumes his old acquaintances of the company; but he saw Kripps, the stage-manager, in the centre of the stage, perspiring and in his shirt-sleeves as always, wildly waving an arm to some one in the flies, and beckoning with the other to the gas-man in the front entrance. The stage hands were striking the scene for the first act, and fighting with the set for the second, and dragging out a canvas floor of tessellated marble, and running a throne and a practical pair of steps over it, and aiming the high quaking walls of a palace and abuse at whoever came in their way.

"Now then, Van Bibber," shouted Kripps, with a wild glance of recognition, as the white-and-black figure came towards him, "you know you're the only man in New York who gets behind here to-night. But you can't stay. Lower it, lower it, can't you?" This to the man in the flies. "Any other night goes, but not this night. I can't have it. I—Where is the backing for the centre entrance? Didn't I tell you men—"

Van Bibber dodged two stage hands who were steering a scene at him, stepped over the carpet as it unrolled, and brushed through a group of anxious, whispering chorus people into the quiet of the star's dressing-room.

The star saw him in the long mirror before which he sat, while his dresser tugged at his boots, and threw up his hands desperately.

"Well," he cried, in mock resignation, "are we in it or are we not? Are they in their seats still or have they fled?"

"How are you, John?" said Van Bibber to the dresser. Then he dropped into a big arm-chair in the corner, and got up again with a protesting sigh to light his cigar between the wires around the gas-burner. "Oh, it's going very well. I wouldn't have come around if it wasn't. If the rest of it is as good as the first act, you needn't worry."

Van Bibber's unchallenged freedom behind the scenes had been a source of much comment and perplexity to the members of the Lester Comic Opera Company. He had made his first appearance there during one hot night of the long run of the previous summer, and had continued to be an almost nightly visitor for several weeks. At first it was supposed that he was backing the piece, that he was the "Angel," as those weak and wealthy individuals are called who allow themselves to be led into supplying the finances for theatrical experiments. But as he never peered through the curtain-hole to count the house, nor made frequent trips to the front of it to look at the box sheet, but was, on the contrary, just as undisturbed on a rainy night as on those when the "standing room only" sign blocked the front entrance, this supposition was discarded as untenable. Nor did he show the least interest in the prima donna, or in any of the other pretty women of the company; he did not know them, nor did he make any effort to know them, and it was not until they inquired concerning him outside of the theatre that they learned what a figure in the social life of the city he really was. He spent most of his time in Lester's dressing-room smoking, listening to the reminiscences of Lester's dresser when Lester was on the stage; and this seclusion and his clerical attire of evening dress led the second comedian to call him Lester's father confessor, and to suggest that he came to the theatre only to take the star to task for his sins. And in this the second comedian was unknowingly not so very far wrong. Lester, the comedian, and young Van Bibber had known each other at the university, when Lester's voice and gift of mimicry had made him the leader in the college theatricals; and later, when he had gone upon the stage, and had been cut off by his family even after he had become famous, or on account of it, Van Bibber had gone to visit him, and had found him as simple and sincere and boyish as he had been in the days of his Hasty-Pudding successes. And Lester, for his part, had found Van Bibber as likable as did every one else, and welcomed his quiet voice and youthful knowledge of the world as a grateful relief to the boisterous *camaraderie* of his professional acquaintances. And he allowed Van Bibber to scold him, and to remind him of what he owed to himself, and to touch, even whether it hurt or not, upon his better side. And in time he admitted to finding his friend's occasional comments on stage matters of value as coming from the point of view of those who look on at the game; and even Kripps, the veteran, regarded him with respect after he had told him that he could turn a set of purple costumes black by throwing a red light on them. To the company, after he came to know them, he was gravely polite, and, to those who knew him if they had overheard, amusingly commonplace in his conversation. He understood them better than they did themselves, and made no mistakes. The women smiled on him, but the men were suspicious and shy of him until they saw that he was quite as shy of the women; and then they made him a confidant, and told him all their woes and troubles, and exhibited all their little jealousies and ambitions, in the innocent hope that he would repeat what they said to Lester. They were simple, unconventional, light-hearted folk, and Van Bibber found them vastly more entertaining and preferable to the silence of the deserted club, where the matting was down, and from whence the regular *habitués* had departed to the other side or to Newport. He liked the swing of the light, bright music as it came to him through the open door of the dressing-room, and the glimpse he got of the chorus people crowding and pushing for a quick charge up the iron stairway, and the feverish smell of oxygen in the air, and the picturesque disorder of Lester's wardrobe, and the wigs and swords, and the mysterious articles of make-up, all mixed together on a tray with half-finished cigars and autograph books and newspaper "notices."

And he often wished he was clever enough to be an artist with the talent to paint the unconsciously graceful groups in the sharply divided light and shadow of the wings as he saw them. The brilliantly colored, fantastically clothed girls leaning against the bare brick wall of the theatre, or whispering together in circles, with their arms close about one another, or reading apart and solitary, or working at some piece of fancy-work as soberly as though they were in a rocking-chair in their own flat, and not leaning against a scene brace, with the glare of the stage and the applause of the house just behind them. He liked to watch them coquetting with the big fireman detailed from the precinct engine-house, and clinging desperately to the curtain wire, or with one of the chorus men on the stairs, or teasing the phlegmatic scene-shifters as they tried to catch a minute's sleep on a pile of canvas. He even forgave the prima donna's smiling at him from the stage, as he stood watching her from the wings, and smiled back at her with polite cynicism, as though he did not know and she did not know that her smiles were not for him, but to disturb some more interested one in the front row. And so, in time, the company became so well accustomed to him that he moved in and about as unnoticed as the stage-manager himself, who prowled around hissing "hush" on principle, even though he was the only person who could fairly be said to be making a noise.

The second act was on, and Lester came off the stage and ran to the dressing-room and beckoned violently. "Come here," he said; "you ought to see this; the children are doing their turn. You want to hear them. They're great!"

Van Bibber put his cigar into a tumbler and stepped out into the wings. They were crowded on both sides of the stage with the members of the company; the girls were tiptoeing, with their hands on the shoulders of the men, and making futile little leaps into the air to get a better view, and others were resting on one knee that those behind might see over their shoulders. There were over a dozen children before the footlights, with the prima donna in the centre. She was singing the verses of a song, and they were following her movements, and joining in the chorus with high piping voices. They seemed entirely too much at home and too self-conscious to please Van Bibber; but there was one exception. The one exception was the smallest of them, a very, very little girl, with long auburn hair and black eyes; such a very little girl that every one in the house looked at her first, and then looked at no one else. She was apparently as unconcerned to all about her, excepting the pretty prima donna, as though she were by a piano at home practising a singing lesson. She seemed to think it was some new sort of a game. When the prima donna raised her arms, the child raised hers; when the prima donna courtesied, she stumbled into one, and straightened herself just in time to get the curls out of her eyes, and to see that the prima donna was laughing at her, and to smile cheerfully back, as if to say, "*We* are doing our best anyway, aren't we?" She had big, gentle eyes and two wonderful dimples, and in the excitement of the dancing and the singing her eyes laughed and flashed, and the dimples deepened and disappeared and reappeared again. She was as happy and innocent looking as though it were nine in the morning and she were playing school at a kindergarten. From all over the house the women were murmuring their delight, and the men were laughing and pulling their mustaches and nudging each other to "look at the littlest one."

The girls in the wings were rapturous in their enthusiasm, and were calling her absurdly extravagant titles of endearment, and making so much noise that Kripps stopped grinning at her from the entrance, and looked back over his shoulder as he looked when he threatened fines and calls for early rehearsal. And when she had finished finally, and the prima donna and the children ran off together, there was a roar from the house that went to Lester's head like wine, and seemed to leap clear across the footlights and drag the children back again.

"That settles it!" cried Lester, in a suppressed roar of triumph. "I knew that child would catch them."

There were four encores, and then the children and Elise Broughten, the pretty prima donna, came off jubilant and happy, with the Littlest Girl's arms full of flowers, which the management had with kindly forethought prepared for the prima donna, but which that delightful young person and the delighted leader of the orchestra had passed over to the little girl.

"Well," gasped Miss Broughten, as she came up to Van Bibber laughing, and with one hand on her side and breathing very quickly, "will you kindly tell me who is the leading woman now? Am I the prima donna, or am I not? I wasn't in it, was I?"

"You were not," said Van Bibber.

He turned from the pretty prima donna and hunted up the wardrobe woman, and told her he wanted to meet the Littlest Girl. And the wardrobe woman, who was fluttering wildly about, and as delighted as though they were all her own children, told him to come into the property-room, where the children were, and which had been changed into a dressing-room that they might be by themselves. The six little girls were in six different states of dishabille, but they were too little to mind that, and Van Bibber was too polite to observe it.

"This is the little girl, sir," said the wardrobe woman, excitedly, proud at being the means of bringing together two such prominent people. "Her name is Madeline. Speak to the gentleman, Madeline; he wants to tell you what a great big hit youse made."

The little girl was seated on one of the cushions of a double throne so high from the ground that the young woman who was pulling off the child's silk stockings and putting woollen ones on in their place did so without stooping. The young woman looked at Van Bibber and nodded somewhat doubtfully and ungraciously, and Van Bibber turned to the little girl in preference. The young woman's face was one of a type that was too familiar to be pleasant.

He took the Littlest Girl's small hand in his and shook it solemnly, and said, "I am very glad to know you. Can I sit up here beside you, or do you rule alone?"

"Yes, ma'am—yes, sir," answered the little girl.

Van Bibber put his hands on the arms of the throne and vaulted up beside the girl, and pulled out the flower in his button-hole and gave it to her.

"Now," prompted the wardrobe woman, "what do you say to the gentleman?"

"Thank you, sir," stammered the little girl.

"She is not much used to gentlemen's society," explained the woman who was pulling on the stockings.

"I see," said Van Bibber. He did not know exactly what to say next. And yet he wanted to talk to the child very much, so much more than he generally wanted to talk to most young women, who showed no hesitation in talking to him. With them he had no difficulty whatsoever. There was a doll lying on the top of a chest near them, and he picked this up and surveyed it critically. "Is this your doll?" he asked.

"No," said Madeline, pointing to one of the children, who was much taller than herself; "it's 'at 'ittle durl's. My doll he's dead."

"Dear me!" said Van Bibber. He made a mental note to get a live one in the morning, and then he said: "That's very sad. But dead dolls do come to life."

The little girl looked up at him, and surveyed him intently and critically, and then smiled, with the dimples showing, as much as to say that she understood him and approved of him entirely. Van Bibber answered this sign language by taking Madeline's hand in his and asking her how she liked being a great actress, and how soon she would begin to storm because *that* photographer hadn't sent the proofs. The young woman understood this, and deigned to smile at it, but Madeline yawned a very polite and sleepy yawn, and closed her eyes. Van Bibber moved up closer, and she leaned over until her bare shoulder touched his arm, and while the woman buttoned on her absurdly small shoes, she let her curly head fall on his elbow and rest there. Any number of people had shown confidence in Van Bibber—not in that form exactly, but in the same spirit—and though he was used to being trusted, he felt a sharp thrill of pleasure at the touch of the child's head on his arm, and in the warm clasp of her fingers around his. And he was conscious of a keen sense of pity and sorrow for her rising in him, which he crushed by thinking that it was entirely wasted, and that the child was probably perfectly and ignorantly happy.

"Look at that, now," said the wardrobe woman, catching sight of the child's closed eyelids; "just look at the rest of the little dears, all that excited they can't stand still to get their hats on, and she just as unconcerned as you please, and after making the hit of the piece, too."

"She's not used to it, you see," said the young woman, knowingly; "she don't know what it means. It's just that much play to her."

This last was said with a questioning glance at Van Bibber, in whom she still feared to find the disguised agent of a Children's Aid Society. Van Bibber only nodded in reply, and did not answer her, because he found he could not very well, for he was looking a long way ahead at what the future was to bring to the confiding little being at his side, and of the evil knowledge and temptations that would mar the beauty of her quaintly sweet face, and its strange mark of gentleness and refinement. Outside he could bear his friend

Lester shouting the refrain of his new topical song, and the laughter and the hand-clapping came in through the wings and open door, broken but tumultuous.

"Does she come of professional people?" Van Bibber asked, dropping into the vernacular. He spoke softly, not so much that he might not disturb the child, but that she might not understand what he said.

"Yes," the woman answered, shortly, and bent her head to smooth out the child's stage dress across her knees.

Van Bibber touched the little girl's head with his hand and found that she was asleep, and so let his hand rest there, with the curls between his fingers. "Are—are you her mother?" he asked, with a slight inclination of his head. He felt quite confident she was not; at least, he hoped not.

The woman shook her head. "No," she said.

"Who is her mother?"

The woman looked at the sleeping child and then up at him almost defiantly. "Ida Clare was her mother," she said.

Van Bibber's protecting hand left the child as suddenly as though something had burned it, and he drew back so quickly that her head slipped from his arm, and she awoke and raised her eyes and looked up at him questioningly. He looked back at her with a glance of the strangest concern and of the deepest pity. Then he stooped and drew her towards him very tenderly, put her head back in the corner of his arm, and watched her in silence while she smiled drowsily and went to sleep again.

"And who takes care of her now?" he asked.

The woman straightened herself and seemed relieved. She saw that the stranger had recognized the child's pedigree and knew her story, and that he was not going to comment on it. "I do," she said. "After the divorce Ida came to me," she said, speaking more freely. "I used to be in her company when she was doing 'Aladdin,' and then when I left the stage and started to keep an actors' boarding-house, she came to me. She lived on with us a year, until she died, and she made me the guardian of the child. I train children for the stage, you know, me and my sister, Ada Dyer; you've heard of her, I guess. The courts pay us for her keep, but it isn't much, and I'm expecting to get what I spent on her from what she makes on the stage. Two of them other children are my pupils; but they can't touch Madie. She is a better dancer an' singer than any of them. If it hadn't been for the Society keeping her back, she would have been on the stage two years ago. She's great, she is. She'll be just as good as her mother was."

Van Bibber gave a little start, and winced visibly, but turned it off into a cough. "And her father," he said, hesitatingly, "does he—"

"Her father," said the woman, tossing back her head, "he looks after himself, he does. We don't ask no favors of *him*. She'll get along without him or his folks, thank you. Call him a gentleman? Nice gentleman he is!" Then she stopped abruptly. "I guess, though, you know him," she added. "Perhaps he's a friend of yourn?"

"I just know him," said Van Bibber, wearily.

He sat with the child asleep beside him while the woman turned to the others and dressed them for the third act. She explained that Madie would not appear in the last act, only the two larger girls, so she let her sleep, with the cape of Van Bibber's cloak around her.

Van Bibber sat there for several long minutes thinking, and then looked up quickly, and dropped his eyes again as quickly, and said, with an effort to speak quietly and unconcernedly: "If the little girl is not on in this act, would you mind if I took her home? I have a cab at the stage-door, and she's so sleepy it seems a pity to keep her up. The sister you spoke of or some one could put her to bed."

"Yes," the woman said, doubtfully, "Ada's home. Yes, you can take her around, if you want to."

She gave him the address, and he sprang down to the floor, and gathered the child up in his arms and stepped out on the stage. The prima donna had the centre of it to herself at that moment, and all the rest of the company were waiting to go on; but when they saw the little girl in Van Bibber's arms they made a rush at her, and the girls leaned over and kissed her with a great show of rapture and with many gasps of delight.

"Don't," said Van Bibber, he could not tell just why. "Don't."

"Why not?" asked one of the girls, looking up at him sharply.

"She was asleep; you've wakened her," he said, gently.

But he knew that was not the reason. He stepped into the cab at the stage entrance, and put the child carefully down in one corner. Then he looked back over his shoulder to see that there was no one near enough to hear him, and said to the driver, "To the Berkeley Flats, on Fifth Avenue." He picked the child up gently in his arms as the carriage started, and sat looking out thoughtfully and anxiously as they flashed past the lighted shop-windows on Broadway. He was far from certain of this errand, and nervous with doubt, but he reassured himself that he was acting on impulse, and that his impulses were so often good. The hall-boy at the Berkeley said, yes, Mr. Caruthers was in, and Van Bibber gave a quick sigh of relief. He took this as an omen that his impulse was a good one. The young English servant who opened the hall door to Mr. Caruthers's apartment suppressed his surprise with an effort, and watched Van Bibber with alarm as he laid the child on the divan in the hall, and pulled a covert coat from the rack to throw over her.

"Just say Mr. Van Bibber would like to see him," he said, "and you need not speak of the little girl having come with me."

She was still sleeping, and Van Bibber turned down the light in the hall, and stood looking down at her gravely while the servant went to speak to his master.

"Will you come this way, please, sir?" he said.

"You had better stay out here," said Van Bibber, "and come and tell me if she wakes."

Mr. Caruthers was standing by the mantel over the empty fireplace, wrapped in a long, loose dressing-gown which he was tying around him as Van Bibber entered. He was partly undressed, and had been just on the point of getting into bed. Mr. Caruthers was a tall, handsome man, with dark reddish hair, turning below the temples into gray; his moustache was quite white, and his eyes and face showed the signs of either dissipation or of great trouble, or of both. But even in the formless dressing-gown he had the look and the confident bearing of a gentleman, or, at least, of the man of the world. The room was very rich-looking, and was filled with the medley of a man's choice of good paintings and fine china, and papered with irregular rows of original drawings and signed etchings. The windows were open, and the lights were turned very low, so that Van Bibber could see the many gas lamps and the dark roofs of Broadway and the Avenue where they crossed a few blocks off, and the bunches of light on the Madison Square Garden, and to the lights on the boats of the East River. From below in the streets came the rattle of hurrying omnibuses and the rush of the hansom cabs. If Mr. Caruthers was surprised at this late visit, he hid it, and came forward to receive his caller as if his presence were expected.

"Excuse my costume, will you?" he said. "I turned in rather early to-night, it was so hot." He pointed to a decanter and some soda bottles on the table and a bowl of ice, and asked, "Will you have some of this?" And while he opened one of the bottles, he watched Van Bibber's face as though he were curious to have him explain the object of his visit.

"No, I think not, thank you," said the younger man. He touched his forehead with his handkerchief nervously. "Yes, it is hot," he said.

Mr. Caruthers filled a glass with ice and brandy and soda, and walked back to his place by the mantel, on which he rested his arm, while he clinked the ice in the glass and looked down into it.

"I was at the first night of 'The Sultana' this evening," said Van Bibber, slowly and uncertainly.

"Oh, yes," assented the elder man, politely, and tasting his drink. "Lester's new piece. Was it any good?"

"I don't know," said Van Bibber. "Yes, I think it was. I didn't see it from the front. There were a lot of children in it—little ones; they danced and sang, and made a great hit. One of them had never been on the stage before. It was her first appearance."

He was turning one of the glasses around between his fingers as he spoke. He stopped, and poured out some of the soda, and drank it down in a gulp, and then continued turning the empty glass between the tips of his fingers.

"It seems to me," he said, "that it is a great pity." He looked up interrogatively at the other man, but Mr. Caruthers met his glance without any returning show of interest. "I say," repeated Van Bibber—"I say it seems a pity that a child like that should be allowed to go on in that business. A grown woman can go into it with her eyes open, or a girl who has had decent training can too. But it's different with a child. She has no choice in the matter; they don't ask her permission; and she isn't old enough to know what it means; and she gets used to it and fond of it before she grows to know what the danger is. And then it's too late. It seemed to me that if there was any one who had a right to stop it, it would be a very good thing to let that person know about her—about this child, I mean; the one who made the hit—before it was too late. It seems to me a responsibility I wouldn't care to take myself. I wouldn't care to think that I had the chance to stop it, and had let the chance go by. You know what the life is, and what the temptation a woman—" Van Bibber stopped with a gasp of concern, and added, hurriedly, "I mean we all know—every man knows."

Mr. Caruthers was looking at him with his lips pressed closely together, and his eyebrows drawn into the shape of the letter V. He leaned forward, and looked at Van Bibber intently.

"What is all this about?" he asked. "Did you come here, Mr. Van Bibber, simply to tell me this? What have you to do with it? What have I to do with it? Why did you come?"

"Because of the child."

"What child?"

"Your child." said Van Bibber.

Young Van Bibber was quite prepared for an outbreak of some sort, and mentally braced himself to receive it. He rapidly assured himself that this man had every reason to be angry, and that he, if he meant to accomplish anything, had every reason to be considerate and patient. So he faced Mr. Caruthers with shoulders squared, as though it were a physical shock he had to stand against, and in consequence he was quite unprepared for what followed. For Mr. Caruthers raised his face without a trace of feeling in it, and, with his eyes still fixed on the glass in his hand, set it carefully down on the mantel beside him, and girded himself about with the rope of his robe. When he spoke, it was in a tone of quiet politeness.

"Mr. Van Bibber," he began, "you are a very brave young man. You have dared to say to me what those who are my best friends—what even my own family would not care to say. They are afraid it might hurt me, I suppose. They have some absurd regard for my feelings; they hesitate to touch upon a subject which in no way concerns them, and which they know must be very painful to me. But you have the courage of your convictions; you have no compunctions about tearing open old wounds; and you come here, unasked and uninvited, to let me know what you think of my conduct, to let me understand that it does not agree with your own ideas of what I ought to do, and to tell me how I, who am old enough to be your father, should behave. You have rushed in where angels fear to tread, Mr. Van Bibber, to show me the error of my ways. I suppose I ought to thank you for it; but I have always said that it is not the wicked people who are to be feared in this world, or who do the most harm. We know them; we can prepare for them, and checkmate them. It is the well-meaning fool who makes all the trouble. For no one knows him until he discloses himself, and the mischief is done before he can be stopped. I think, if you will allow me to say so, that you have demonstrated my theory pretty thoroughly and have done about as much needless harm for one evening as you can possibly wish. And so, if you will excuse me," he continued, sternly, and moving from his place, "I will ask to say good-night, and will request of you that you grow older and wiser and much more considerate before you come to see me again."

Van Bibber had flushed at Mr. Caruthers's first words, and had then grown somewhat pale, and straightened himself visibly. He did not move when the elder man had finished, but cleared his throat, and then spoke with some little difficulty. "It is very easy to call a man a fool," he said, slowly, "but it is much harder to be called a fool and not to throw the other man out of the window. But that, you see, would not do any good, and I have something to say to you first. I am quite clear in my own mind as to my position, and I am not going to allow anything you have said or can say to annoy me much until I am through. There will be time enough to resent it then. I am quite well aware that I did an unconventional thing in coming here—a bold thing or a foolish thing, as you choose—but the situation is pretty bad, and I did as I would have wished to be done by if I had had a child going to the devil and didn't know it. I should have been glad to learn of it even from a stranger. However," he said, smiling grimly, and pulling his cape about him, "there are other kindly disposed people in the world besides fathers. There is an aunt, perhaps, or an uncle or two; and sometimes, even to-day, there is the chance Samaritan."

Van Bibber picked up his high hat from the table, looked into it critically, and settled it on his head. "Good-night," he said, and walked slowly towards the door. He had his hand on the knob, when Mr. Caruthers raised his head.

"Wait just one minute, please, Mr. Van Bibber?" asked Mr. Caruthers.

Van Bibber stopped with a prompt obedience which would have led one to conclude that be might have put on his hat only to precipitate matters.

"Before you go," said Mr. Caruthers, grudgingly, "I want to say—I want you to understand my position."

"Oh, that's all right," said Van Bibber, lightly, opening the door.

"No, it is not all right. One moment, please. I do not intend that you shall go away from here with the idea that you have tried to do me a service, and that I have been unable to appreciate it, and that you are a much-abused and much-misunderstood young man. Since you have done me the honor to make my affairs your business, I would prefer that you should understand them fully. I do not care to have you discuss my conduct at clubs and afternoon teas with young women until you—"

Van Bibber drew in his breath sharply, with a peculiar whistling sound, and opened and shut his hands. "Oh, I wouldn't say that if I were you," he said, simply.

"I beg your pardon," the older man said, quickly. "That was a mistake. I was wrong. I beg your pardon. But you have tried me very sorely. You have intruded upon a private trouble that you ought to know must be very painful to me. But I believe you meant well. I know you to be a gentleman, and I am willing to think you acted on impulse, and that you will see to-morrow what a mistake you have made. It is not a thing I talk about; I do not speak of it to my friends, and they are far too considerate to speak of it to me. But you have put me on the defensive. You have made me out more or less of a brute, and I don't intend to be so far misunderstood. There are two sides to every story, and there is something to be said about this, even for me."

He walked back to his place beside the mantel, and put his shoulders against it, and faced Van Bibber, with his fingers twisted in the cord around his waist.

"When I married," said Mr. Caruthers, "I did so against the wishes of my people and the advice of all my friends. You know all about that. God help us! who doesn't?" he added, bitterly. "It was very rich, rare reading for you and for every one else who saw the daily papers, and we gave them all they wanted of it. I took her out of that life and married her because I believed she was as good a woman as any of those who had never had to work for their living, and I was bound that my friends and your friends should recognize her and respect her as my wife had a right to be respected; and I took her abroad that I might give all you sensitive, fine people a chance to get used to the idea of being polite to a woman who had once been a burlesque actress. It began over there in Paris. What I went through then no one knows; but when I came back—and I would never have come back if she had not made me—it was my friends I had to consider, and not her. It was in the blood; it was in the life she had led, and in the life men like you and me had taught her to live. And it had to come out."

The muscles of Mr. Caruthers's face were moving, and beyond his control; but Van Bibber did not see this, for he was looking intently out of the window, over the roofs of the city.

"She had every chance when she married me that a woman ever had," continued the older man. "It only depended on herself. I didn't try to make a housewife of her or a drudge. She had all the healthy excitement and all the money she wanted, and she had a home here ready for her whenever she was tired of travelling about and wished to settle down. And I was—and a husband that loved her as—she had everything. Everything that a man's whole thought and love and money could bring to her. And you know what she did."

He looked at Van Bibber, but Van Bibber's eyes were still turned towards the open window and the night.

"And after the divorce—and she was free to go where she pleased, and to live as she pleased and with whom she pleased, without bringing disgrace on a husband who honestly loved her—I swore to my God that I would never see her nor her child again. And I never saw her again, not even when she died. I loved the mother, and she deceived me and disgraced me and broke my heart, and I only wish she had killed me; and I was beginning to love her child, and I vowed she should not live to trick me too. I had suffered as no man I know had suffered; in a way a boy like you cannot understand, and that no one can understand who has not gone to hell and been forced to live after it. And was I to go through that again? Was I to love and care for and worship this child, and have her grow up with all her mother's vanity and animal nature, and have her turn on me some day and show me that what is bred in the bone must tell, and that I was a fool again—a pitiful fond fool? I could not trust her. I can never trust any woman or child again, and least of all that woman's child. She is as dead to me as though she were buried with her mother, and it is nothing to me what she is or what her life is. I know in time what it will be. She has begun earlier than I had supposed, that is all; but she is nothing to me." The man stopped and turned his back to Van Bibber, and hid his head in his hands, with his elbows on the mantel-piece. "I care too much," he said. "I cannot let it mean anything to me; when I do care, it means so much more to me than to other men. They may pretend to laugh and to forget and to outgrow it, but it is not so with me. It means too much." He took a quick stride towards one of the arm-chairs, and threw himself into it. "Why, man," he cried, "I loved that child's mother to the day of her death. I loved that woman then, and, God help me! I love that woman still."

He covered his face with his hands, and sat leaning forward and breathing heavily as he rocked himself to and fro. Van Bibber still stood looking gravely out at the lights that picketed the black surface of the city. He was to all appearances as unmoved by the outburst of feeling into which the older man had been surprised as though it had been something in a play. There was an unbroken silence for a moment, and then it was Van Bibber who was the first to speak.

"I came here, as you say, on impulse," he said; "but I am glad I came, for I have your decisive answer now about the little girl. I have been thinking," he continued, slowly, "since you have been speaking, and before, when I first saw her dancing in front of the footlights, when I did not know who she was, that I could give up a horse or two, if necessary, and support this child instead. Children are worth more than horses, and a man who saves a soul, as it says"—he flushed slightly, and looked up with a hesitating, deprecatory smile—"somewhere, wipes out a multitude of sins. And it may be I'd like to try and get rid of some of mine. I know just where to send her; I know the very place. It's down in Evergreen Bay, on Long Island. They are tenants of mine there, and very nice farm sort of people, who will be very good to her. They wouldn't know anything about her, and she'd forget what little she knows of this present life very soon, and grow up with the other children to be one of them; and then, when she gets older and becomes a young lady, she could go to some school—but that's a bit too far ahead to plan for the present; but that's what I am going to do, though," said the young man, confidently, and as though speaking to himself. "That theatrical boarding-house person could be bought off easily enough," he went on, quickly, "and Lester won't mind letting her go if I ask it, and—and that's what I'll do. As you say, it's a good deal of an experiment, but I think I'll run the risk."

He walked quickly to the door and disappeared in the hall, and then came back, kicking the door open as he returned, and holding the child in his arms.

"This is she," he said, quietly. He did not look at or notice the father, but stood, with the child asleep in the bend of his left arm, gazing down at her. "This is she," he repeated; "this is your child."

There was something cold and satisfied in Van Bibber's tone and manner, as though he were congratulating himself upon the engaging of a new groom; something that placed the father entirely outside of it. He might have been a disinterested looker-on.

"She will need to be fed a bit," Van Bibber ran on, cheerfully. "They did not treat her very well, I fancy. She is thin and peaked and tired-looking." He drew up the loose sleeve of her jacket, and showed the bare forearm to the light. He put his thumb and little finger about it, and closed them on it gently. "It is very thin," he said. "And under her eyes, if it were not for the paint," he went on, mercilessly, "you could see how deep the lines are. This red spot on her cheek," he said, gravely, "is where Mary Vane kissed her to-night, and this is where Alma Stantley kissed her, and that Lee girl. You have heard of them, perhaps. They will never kiss her again. She is going to grow up a sweet, fine, beautiful woman—are you not?" he said, gently drawing the child higher up on his shoulder, until her face touched his, and still keeping his eyes from the face of the older man. "She does not look like her mother," he said; "she has her father's auburn hair and straight nose and finer-cut lips and chin. She looks very much like her father. It seems a pity," he added, abruptly. "She will grow up," he went on, "without knowing him, or who he is—or was, if he should die. She will never speak with him, or see him, or take his hand. She may pass him some day on the street and will not know him, and he will not know her, but she will grow to be very fond and to be very grateful to the simple, kind-hearted old people who will have cared for her when she was a little girl."

The child in his arms stirred, shivered slightly, and awoke. The two men watched her breathlessly, with silent intentness. She raised her head and stared around the unfamiliar room doubtfully, then turned to where her father stood, looking at him a moment, and passed him by; and then, looking up into Van Bibber's face, recognized him, and gave a gentle, sleepy smile, and, with a sigh of content and confidence, drew her arm up closer around his neck, and let her head fall back upon his breast.

The father sprang to his feet with a quick, jealous gasp of pain. "Give her to me!" he said, fiercely, under his breath, snatching her out of Van Bibber's arms. "She is mine; give her to me!"

Van Bibber closed the door gently behind him, and went jumping down the winding stairs of the Berkeley three steps at a time.

And an hour later, when the English servant came to his master's door, he found him still awake and sitting in the dark by the open window, holding something in his arms and looking out over the sleeping city.

"James," he said, "you can make up a place for me here on the lounge. Miss Caruthers, my daughter, will sleep in my room to-night."

VAN BIBBER'S MAN-SERVANT

Van Bibber's man Walters was the envy and admiration of his friends. He was English, of course, and he had been trained in the household of the Marquis Bendinot, and had travelled, in his younger days, as the valet of young Lord Upton. He was now rather well on in years, although it would have been impossible to say just how old he was. Walters had a dignified and repellent air about him, and he brushed his hair in such a way as to conceal his baldness.

And when a smirking, slavish youth with red cheeks and awkward gestures turned up in Van Bibber's livery, his friends were naturally surprised, and asked how he had come to lose Walters. Van Bibber could not say exactly, at least he could not rightly tell whether he had dismissed Walters or Walters had dismissed himself. The facts of the unfortunate separation were like this:

Van Bibber gave a great many dinners during the course of the season at Delmonico's, dinners hardly formal enough to require a private room, and yet too important to allow of his running the risk of keeping his guests standing in the hall waiting for a vacant table. So he conceived the idea of sending Walters over about half-past six to keep a table for him. As everybody knows, you can hold a table yourself at Delmonico's for any length of time until the other guests arrive, but the rule is very strict about servants. Because, as the head waiter will tell you, if servants were allowed to reserve a table during the big rush at seven o'clock, why not messenger boys? And it would certainly never do to have half a dozen large tables securely held by minute messengers while the hungry and impatient waited their turn at the door.

But Walters looked as much like a gentleman as did many of the diners; and when he seated himself at the largest table and told the waiter to serve for a party of eight or ten; he did it with such an air that the head waiter came over himself and took the orders. Walters knew quite as much about ordering a dinner as did his master; and when Van Bibber was too tired to make out the menu, Walters would look over the card himself and order the proper wines and side dishes; and with such a carelessly severe air and in such a masterly manner did he discharge this high function that the waiters looked upon him with much respect.

But respect even from your equals and the satisfaction of having your fellow-servants mistake you for a member of the Few Hundred are not enough. Walters wanted more. He wanted the further satisfaction of enjoying the delicious dishes he had ordered; of sitting as a coequal with the people for whom he had kept a place; of completing the deception he practised only up to the point where it became most interesting.

It certainly was trying to have to rise with a subservient and unobtrusive bow and glide out unnoticed by the real guests when they arrived; to have to relinquish the feast just when the feast should begin. It would not be pleasant, certainly, to sit for an hour at a big empty table, ordering dishes fit only for epicures, and then, just as the waiters bore down with the Little Neck clams, so nicely iced and so cool and bitter-looking, to have to rise and go out into the street to a *table d'hôte* around the corner.

This was Walters's state of mind when Mr. Van Bibber told him for the hundredth time to keep a table for him for three at Delmonico's. Walters wrapped his severe figure in a frock-coat and brushed his hair, and allowed himself the dignity of a walking-stick. He would have liked to act as a substitute in an evening dress-suit, but Van Bibber would not have allowed it. So Walters walked over to Delmonico's and took a table near a window, and said that the other gentlemen would arrive later. Then he looked at his watch and ordered the dinner. It was just the sort of dinner he would have ordered had he ordered it for himself at some one else's expense. He suggested Little Neck clams first, with chablis, and pea-soup, and caviare on toast, before the oyster crabs, with Johannisberger Cabinet; then an *entrée* of calves' brains and rice; then no roast, but a bird, cold asparagus with French dressing, Camembert cheese, and Turkish coffee. As there were to be no women, he omitted the sweets and added three other wines to follow the white wine. It struck him as a particularly well-chosen dinner, and the longer he sat and thought about it the more he wished he were to test its excellence. And then the people all around him were so bright and happy, and seemed to be enjoying what they had ordered with such a refinement of zest that he felt he would give a great deal could he just sit there as one of them for a brief hour.

At that moment the servant deferentially handed him a note which a messenger boy had brought. It said:

"Dinner off called out town send clothes and things after me to Young's Boston.   VAN BIBBER."

Walter rose involuntarily, and then sat still to think about it. He would have to countermand the dinner which he had ordered over half an hour before, and he would have to explain who he was to those other servants who had always regarded him as such a great gentleman. It was very hard.

And then Walters was tempted. He was a very good servant, and he knew his place as only an English servant can, and he had always accepted it, but to-night he was tempted—and he fell. He met the waiter's anxious look with a grave smile.

"The other gentlemen will not be with me to-night," he said, glancing at the note. "But I will dine here as I intended. You can serve for one."

That was perhaps the proudest night in the history of Walters. He had always felt that he was born out of his proper sphere, and to-night he was assured of it. He was a little nervous at first, lest some of Van Bibber's friends should come in and recognize him; but as the dinner progressed and the warm odor of the dishes touched his sense, and the rich wines ran through his veins, and the women around him smiled and bent and moved like beautiful birds of beautiful plumage, he became content, grandly content; and he half closed his eyes and imagined he was giving a dinner to everybody in the place. Vain and idle thoughts came to him and went again, and he eyed the others about him calmly and with polite courtesy, as they did him, and he felt that if he must later pay for this moment it was worth the paying.

Then he gave the waiter a couple of dollars out of his own pocket and wrote Van Bibber's name on the check, and walked in state into the *café*, where he ordered a green mint and a heavy, black, and expensive cigar, and seated himself at the window, where he felt that he should always have sat if the fates had been just. The smoke hung in light clouds about him, and the lights shone and glistened on the white cloths and the broad shirt-fronts of the smart young men and distinguished foreign-looking older men at the surrounding tables.

And then, in the midst of his dreamings, he heard the soft, careless drawl of his master, which sounded at that time and in that place like the awful voice of a condemning judge. Van Bibber pulled out a chair and dropped into it. His side was towards Walters, so that he did not see him. He had some men with him, and he was explaining how he had missed his train and had come back to find that one of the party had eaten the dinner without him, and he wondered who it could be; and then turning easily in his seat he saw Walters with the green mint and the cigar, trembling behind a copy of the London *Graphic.*

"Walters!" said Van Bibber, "what are you doing here?"

Walters looked his guilt and rose stiffly. He began with a feeble "If you please, sir—"

"Go back to my rooms and wait for me there," said Van Bibber, who was too decent a fellow to scold a servant in public.

Walters rose and left the half-finished cigar and the mint with the ice melting in it on the table. His one evening of sublimity was over, and he walked away, bending before the glance of his young master and the smiles of his master's friends.

When Van Bibber came back he found on his dressing-table a note from Walters stating that he could not, of course, expect to remain longer in his service, and that he left behind him the twenty-eight dollars which the dinner had cost.

"If he had only gone off with all my waistcoats and scarf-pins, I'd have liked it better," said Van Bibber, "than his leaving me cash for infernal dinner. Why, a servant like Walters is worth twenty-eight-dollar dinners—twice a day."

THE HUNGRY MAN WAS FED

Young Van Bibber broke one of his rules of life one day and came down-town. This unusual journey into the marts of trade and finance was in response to a call from his lawyer, who wanted his signature to some papers. It was five years since Van Bibber had been south of the north side of Washington Square, except as a transient traveller to the ferries on the elevated road. And as he walked through the City Hall Square he looked about him at the new buildings in the air, and the bustle and confusion of the streets, with as much interest as a lately arrived immigrant.

He rather enjoyed the novelty of the situation, and after he had completed his business at the lawyer's office he tried to stroll along lower Broadway as he did on the Avenue.

But people bumped against him, and carts and drays tried to run him down when he crossed the side streets, and those young men whom he knew seemed to be in a great hurry, and expressed such amused surprise at seeing him that he felt very much out of place indeed. And so he decided to get back to his club window and its quiet as soon as possible.

"Hello, Van Bibber," said one of the young men who were speeding by, "what brings you here? Have you lost your way?"

"I think I have," said Van Bibber. "If you'll kindly tell me how I can get back to civilization again, be obliged to you."

"Take the elevated from Park Place," said his friend from over his shoulder, as he nodded and dived into the crowd.

The visitor from up-town had not a very distinct idea as to where Park Place was, but he struck off Broadway and followed the line of the elevated road along Church Street. It was at the corner of Vesey Street that a miserable-looking, dirty, and red-eyed object stood still in his tracks and begged Van Bibber for a few cents to buy food. "I've come all the way from Chicago," said the Object, "and I haven't tasted food for twenty-four hours."

Van Bibber drew away as though the Object had a contagious disease in his rags, and handed him a quarter without waiting to receive the man's blessing.

"Poor devil!" said Van Bibber. "Fancy going without dinner all day!" He could not fancy this, though he tried, and the impossibility of it impressed him so much that he amiably determined to go back and hunt up the Object and give him more money. Van Bibber's ideas of a dinner were rather exalted. He did not know of places where a quarter was good for a "square meal," including "one roast, three vegetables, and pie." He hardly considered a quarter a sufficiently large tip for the waiter who served the dinner, and decidedly not enough for the dinner itself. He did not see his man at first, and when he did the man did not see him. Van Bibber watched him stop three gentlemen, two of whom gave him some money, and then the Object approached Van Bibber and repeated his sad tale in a monotone. He evidently did not recognize Van Bibber, and the clubman gave him a half-dollar and walked away, feeling that the man must surely have enough by this time with which to get something to eat, if only a luncheon.

This retracing of his footsteps had confused Van Bibber, and he made a complete circuit of the block before he discovered that he had lost his bearings. He was standing just where he had started, and gazing along the line of the elevated road, looking for a station, when the familiar accents of the Object again saluted him.

When Van Bibber faced him the beggar looked uneasy. He was not sure whether or not he had approached this particular gentleman before, but Van Bibber conceived an idea of much subtlety, and deceived the Object by again putting his hand in his pocket.

"Nothing to eat for twenty-four hours! Dear me!" drawled the clubman, sympathetically. "Haven't you any money, either?"

"Not a cent," groaned the Object, "an' I'm just faint for food, sir. S'help me. I hate to beg, sir. It isn't the money I want, it's jest food. I'm starvin', sir."

"Well," said Van Bibber, suddenly, "if it is just something to eat you want, come in here with me and I'll give you your breakfast." But the man held back and began to whine and complain that they wouldn't let the likes of him in such a fine place.

"Oh, yes, they will," said Van Bibber, glancing at the bill of fare in front of the place. "It seems to be extremely cheap. Beefsteak fifteen cents, for instance. Go in," he added, and there was something in his tone which made the Object move ungraciously into the eating-house.

It was a very queer place, Van Bibber thought, and the people stared very hard at him and his gloves and the gardenia in his coat and at the tramp accompanying him.

"You ain't going to eat two breakfasts, are yer?" asked one of the very tough-looking waiters of the Object. The Object looked uneasy, and Van Bibber, who stood beside his chair, smiled in triumph.

"You're mistaken," he said to the waiter. "This gentleman is starving; he has not tasted food for twenty-four hours. Give him whatever he asks for!"

The Object scowled and the waiter grinned behind his tin tray, and had the impudence to wink at Van Bibber, who recovered from this in time to give the man a half-dollar and so to make of him a friend for life. The Object ordered milk, but Van Bibber protested and ordered two beefsteaks and fried potatoes, hot rolls and two omelettes, coffee, and ham with bacon.

"Holy smoke! watcher think I am?" yelled the Object, in desperation.

"Hungry," said Van Bibber, very gently. "Or else an impostor. And, you know, if you should happen to be the latter I should have to hand you over to the police."

Van Bibber leaned easily against the wall and read the signs about him, and kept one eye on a policeman across the street. The Object was choking and cursing through his breakfast. It did not seem to agree with him. Whenever he stopped Van Bibber would point with his stick to a still unfinished dish, and the Object, after a husky protest, would attack it as though it were poison. The people sitting about were laughing, and the proprietor behind the desk smiling grimly.

"There, darn ye!" said the Object at last. "I've eat all I can eat for a year. You think you're mighty smart, don't ye? But if you choose to pay that high for your fun, I s'pose you can afford it. Only don't let me catch you around these streets after dark, that's all."

And the Object started off, shaking his fist.

"Wait a minute," said Van Bibber. "You haven't paid them for your breakfast."

"Haven't what?" shouted the Object. "Paid 'em! How could I pay him? Youse asked me to come in here and eat. I didn't want no breakfast, did I? Youse'll have to pay for your fun yerself, or they'll throw yer out. Don't try to be too smart."

"I gave you," said Van Bibber, slowly, "seventy-five cents with which to buy a breakfast. This check calls for eighty-five cents, and extremely cheap it is," he added, with a bow to the fat proprietor. "Several other gentlemen, on your representation that you were starving, gave you other sums to be expended on a breakfast. You have the money with you now. So pay what you owe at once, or I'll call that officer across the street and tell him what I know, and have you put where you belong."

"I'll see you blowed first!" gasped the Object.

Van Bibber turned to the waiter. "Kindly beckon to that officer," said he.

The waiter ran to the door and the Object ran too, but the tough waiter grabbed him by the back of his neck and held him.

"Lemme go!" yelled the Object. "Lemme go an' I'll pay you."

Everybody in the place came up now and formed a circle around the group and watched the Object count out eighty-five cents into the waiter's hand, which left him just one dime to himself.

"You have forgotten the waiter who served you," said Van Bibber, severely pointing with his stick at the dime.

"No, you don't," groaned the Object.

"Oh, yes," said Van Bibber, "do the decent thing now, or I'll—"

The Object dropped the dime in the waiter's hand, and Van Bibber, smiling and easy, made his way through the admiring crowd and out into the street.

"I suspect," said Mr. Van Bibber later in the day, when recounting his adventure to a fellow-clubman, "that, after I left, fellow tried to get tip back from waiter, for I saw him come out of place very suddenly, you see, and without touching pavement till he lit on back of his head in gutter. He was most remarkable waiter."

VAN BIBBER AT THE RACES

Young Van Bibber had never spent a Fourth of July in the city, as he had always understood it was given over to armies of small boys on that day, who sat on all the curbstones and set off fire-crackers, and that the thermometer always showed ninety degrees in the shade, and cannon boomed and bells rang from daybreak to midnight. He had refused all invitations to join any Fourth-of-July parties at the seashore or on the Sound or at Tuxedo, because he expected his people home from Europe, and had to be in New York to meet them. He was accordingly greatly annoyed when he received a telegram saying they would sail in a boat a week later.

He finished his coffee at the club on the morning of the Fourth about ten o'clock, in absolute solitude, and with no one to expect and nothing to anticipate; so he asked for a morning paper and looked up the amusements offered for the Fourth. There were plenty of excursions with brass bands, and refreshments served on board, baseball matches by the hundred, athletic meetings and picnics by the dozen, but nothing that seemed to exactly please him.

The races sounded attractive, but then he always lost such a lot of money, and the crowd pushed so, and the sun and the excitement made his head ache between the eyes and spoiled his appetite for dinner. He had vowed again and again that he would not go to the races; but as the day wore on and the solitude of the club became oppressive and the silence of the Avenue began to tell on him, he changed his mind, and made his preparations accordingly.

First, he sent out after all the morning papers and read their tips on the probable winners. Very few of them agreed, so he took the horse which most of them seemed to think was best, and determined to back it, no matter what might happen or what new tips he might get later. Then he put two hundred dollars in his pocket-book to bet with, and twenty dollars for expenses, and sent around for his field-glasses.

He was rather late in starting, and he made up his mind on the way to Morris Park that he would be true to the list of winners he had written out, and not make any side bets on any suggestions or inside information given him by others. He vowed a solemn vow on the rail of the boat to plunge on each of the six horses he had selected from the newspaper tips, and on no others. He hoped in this way to win something. He did not care so much to win, but he hated to lose. He always felt so flat and silly after it was over; and when it happened, as it often did, that he had paid several hundred dollars for the afternoon's sport, his sentiments did him credit.

"I shall probably, or rather certainly, be tramped on and shoved," soliloquized Van Bibber.

"I shall smoke more cigars than are good for me, and drink more than I want, owing to the unnatural excitement and heat, and I shall be late for my dinner. And for all this I shall probably pay two hundred dollars. It really seems as if I were a young man of little intellect, and yet thousands of others are going to do exactly the same thing."

The train was very late. One of the men in front said they would probably just be able to get their money up in time for the first race. A horse named Firefly was Van Bibber's choice, and he took one hundred dollars of his two hundred to put up on her. He had it already in his hand when the train reached the track, and he hurried with the rest towards the bookmakers to get his one hundred on as quickly as possible. But while he was crossing the lawn back of the stand, he heard cheers and wild yells that told him they were running the race at that moment.

"Raceland!" "Raceland!" "Raceland by a length!" shouted the crowd.

"Who's second?" a fat man shouted at another fat man.

"Firefly," called back the second, joyously, "and I've got her for a place and I win eight dollars."

"Ah!" said Van Bibber, as he slipped his one hundred dollars back in his pocket, "good thing I got here a bit late."

"What'd you win, Van Bibber?" asked a friend who rushed past him, clutching his tickets as though they were precious stones.

"I win one hundred dollars," answered Van Bibber, calmly, as he walked on up into the boxes. It was delightfully cool up there, and to his satisfaction and surprise he found several people there whom he knew. He went into Her box and accepted some *pâté* sandwiches and iced champagne, and chatted and laughed with Her so industriously, and so much to the exclusion of all else, that the horses were at the starting-post before he was aware of it, and he had to excuse himself hurriedly and run to put up his money on Bugler, the second on his list. He decided that as he had won one hundred dollars on the first race he could afford to plunge on this one, so he counted out fifty more, and putting this with the original one hundred dollars, crowded into the betting-ring and said, "A hundred and fifty on Bugler straight."

"Bugler's just been scratched," said the bookie, leaning over Van Bibber's shoulder for a greasy five-dollar bill.

"Will you play anything else?" he asked, as the young gentleman stood there irresolute.

"No, thank you," said Van Bibber, remembering his vow, and turning hastily away. "Well," he mused, "I'm one hundred and fifty dollars better off than I might have been if Bugler hadn't been scratched and hadn't won. One hundred and fifty dollars added to one hundred makes two hundred and fifty dollars. That puts me 'way ahead of the game. I am fifty dollars better off than when I left New York. I'm playing in great luck." So, on the strength of this, he bought out the man who sells bouquets, and ordered more champagne to be sent up to the box where She was sitting, and they all congratulated him on his winnings, which were suggested by his generous and sudden expenditures.

"You must have a great eye for picking a winner," said one of the older men, grudgingly.

"Y-e-s," said Van Bibber, modestly. "I know a horse when I see it, I think; and," he added to himself, "that's about all."

His horse for the third race was Rover, and the odds were five to one against him. Van Bibber wanted very much to bet on Pirate King instead, but he remembered his vow to keep to the list he had originally prepared, whether he lost or won. This running after strange gods was always a losing business. He took one hundred dollars in five-dollar bills, and went down to the ring and put the hundred up on Rover and returned to the box. The horses had been weighed in and the bugle had sounded, and three of the racers were making their way up the track, when one of them plunged suddenly forward and went down on his knees and then stretched out dead. Van Bibber was confident it was Rover, although he had no idea which the horse was, but he knew his horse would not run. There was a great deal of excitement, and people who did not know the rule, which requires the return of all money if any accident happens to a horse on the race-track between the time of weighing in and arriving at the post, were needlessly alarmed. Van Bibber walked down to the ring and received his money back with a smile.

"I'm just one hundred dollars better off than I was three minutes ago," he said. "I've really had a most remarkable day."

Mayfair was his choice for the fourth race, and she was selling at three to one. Van Bibber determined to put one hundred and seventy-five dollars up on her, for, as he said, he had not lost on any one race yet. The girl in the box was very interesting, though, and Van Bibber found a great deal to say to her. He interrupted himself once to call to one of the messenger-boys who ran with bets, and gave him one hundred and seventy-five dollars to put on Mayfair.

Several other gentlemen gave the boy large sums as well, and Van Bibber continued to talk earnestly with the girl. He raised his head to see Mayfair straggle in a bad second, and shrugged his shoulders. "How much did you lose?" she asked.

"Oh, 'bout two hundred dollars," said Van Bibber; "but it's the first time I've lost to-day, so I'm still ahead." He bent over to continue what he was saying, when a rude commotion and loud talking caused those in the boxes to raise their heads and look around. Several gentlemen were pointing out Van Bibber to one of the Pinkerton detectives, who had a struggling messenger-boy in his grasp.

"These gentlemen say you gave this boy some money, sir," said the detective. "He tried to do a welsh with it, and I caught him just as he was getting over the fence. How much and on what horse, sir?"

Van Bibber showed his memoranda, and the officer handed him over one hundred and seventy-five dollars.

"Now, let me see," said Van Bibber, shutting one eye and calculating intently, "one hundred and seventy-five to three hundred and fifty dollars makes me a winner by five hundred and twenty-five dollars. That's purty good, isn't it? I'll have a great dinner at Delmonico's to-night. You'd better all come back with me!"

But She said he had much better come back with her and her party on top of the coach and take dinner in the cool country instead of the hot, close city, and Van Bibber said he would like to, only he did wish to get his one hundred dollars up on at least one race. But they said "no," they must be off at once, for the ride was a long one, and Van Bibber looked at his list and saw that his choice was Jack Frost, a very likely winner, indeed; but, nevertheless, he walked out to the enclosure with them and mounted the coach beside the girl on the back seat, with only the two coachmen behind to hear what he chose to say.

And just as they finally were all harnessed up and the horn sounded, the crowd yelled, "They're off," and Van Bibber and all of them turned on their high seats to look back.

"Magpie wins," said the whip.

"And Jack Frost's last," said another.

"And I win my one hundred dollars," said Van Bibber. "It's really very curious," he added, turning to the girl. "I started out with two hundred dollars to-day, I spent only twenty-five dollars on flowers, I won six hundred and twenty-five dollars, and I have only one hundred and seventy-five dollars to show for it, and yet I've had a very pleasant Fourth."

AN EXPERIMENT IN ECONOMY

Of course, Van Bibber lost all the money he saved at the races on the Fourth of July. He went to the track the next day, and he saw the whole sum melt away, and in his vexation tried to "get back," with the usual result. He plunged desperately, and when he had reached his rooms and run over his losses, he found he was a financial wreck, and that he, as his sporting friends expressed it, "would have to smoke a pipe" for several years to come, instead of indulging in Regalias. He could not conceive how he had come to make such a fool of himself, and he wondered if he would have enough confidence to spend a dollar on luxuries again.

It was awful to contemplate the amount he had lost. He felt as if it were sinful extravagance to even pay his car-fare up-town, and he contemplated giving his landlord the rent with keen distress. It almost hurt him to part with five cents to the conductor, and as he looked at the hansoms dashing by with lucky winners inside he groaned audibly.

"I've got to economize," he soliloquized. "No use talking; must economize. I'll begin to-morrow morning and keep it up for a month. Then I'll be on my feet again. Then I can stop economizing, and enjoy myself. But no more races; never, never again."

He was delighted with this idea of economizing. He liked the idea of self-punishment that it involved, and as he had never denied himself anything in his life, the novelty of the idea charmed him. He rolled over to sleep, feeling very much happier in his mind than he had been before his determination was taken, and quite eager to begin on the morrow. He arose very early, about ten o'clock, and recalled his idea of economy for a month, as a saving clause to his having lost a month's spending money.

He was in the habit of taking his coffee and rolls and a parsley omelette, at Delmonico's every morning. He decided that he would start out on his road of economy by omitting the omelette and ordering only a pot of coffee. By some rare intuition he guessed that there were places up-town where things were cheaper than at his usual haunt, only he did not know where they were. He stumbled into a restaurant on a side street finally, and ordered a cup of coffee and some rolls.

The waiter seemed to think that was a very poor sort of breakfast, and suggested some nice chops or a bit of steak or "ham and eggs, sah," all of which made Van Bibber shudder. The waiter finally concluded that Van Bibber was poor and couldn't afford any more, which, as it happened to be more or less true, worried that young gentleman; so much so, indeed, that when the waiter brought him a check for fifteen cents, Van Bibber handed him a half-dollar and told him to "keep the change."

The satisfaction he felt in this wore off very soon when he appreciated that, while he had economized in his breakfast, his vanity had been very extravagantly pampered, and he felt how absurd it was when he remembered he would not have spent more if he had gone to Delmonico's in the first place. He wanted one of those large black Regalias very much, but they cost entirely too much. He went carefully through his pockets to see if he had one with him, but he had not, and he determined to get a pipe. Pipes are always cheap.

"What sort of a pipe, sir?" said the man behind the counter.

"A cheap pipe," said Van Bibber.

"But what sort?" persisted the man.

Van Bibber thought a brier pipe, with an amber mouth-piece and a silver band, would about suit his fancy. The man had just such a pipe, with trade-marks on the brier and hall-marks and "Sterling" on the silver band. It lay in a very pretty silk box, and there was another mouth-piece you could screw in, and a cleaner and top piece with which to press the tobacco down. It was most complete, and only five dollars. "Isn't that a good deal for a pipe?" asked Van Bibber. The man said, being entirely unprejudiced, that he thought not. It was cheaper, he said, to get a good thing at the start. It lasted longer. And cheap pipes bite your tongue. This seemed to Van Bibber most excellent reasoning. Some Oxford-Cambridge mixture attracted Van Bibber on account of its name. This cost one dollar more. As he left the shop he saw a lot of pipes, brier and corn-cob and Sallie Michaels, in the window marked, "Any of these for a quarter." This made him feel badly, and he was conscious he was not making a success of his economy. He started back to the club, but it was so hot that he thought he would faint before he got there; so he called a hansom, on the principle that it was cheaper to ride and keep well than to walk and have a sunstroke.

He saw some people that he knew going by in a cab with a pile of trunks on the top of it, and that reminded him that they had asked him to come down and see them off when the steamer left that afternoon. So he waved his hand when they passed, and bowed to them, and cried, "See you later," before he counted the consequences. He did not wish to arrive empty-handed, so he stopped in at a florist's and got a big basket of flowers and another of fruit, and piled them into the hansom.

When be came to pay the driver he found the trip from Thirty-fifth Street to the foot of Liberty was two dollars and a half, and the fruit and flowers came to twenty-two dollars. He was greatly distressed over this, and could not see how it had happened. He rode back in the elevated for five cents and felt much better. Then some men just back from a yachting trip joined him at the club and ordered a great many things to drink, and of course he had to do the same, and seven dollars were added to his economy fund. He argued that this did not matter, because he signed a check for it, and that he would not have to pay for it until the end of the month, when the necessity of economizing would be over.

Still, his conscience did not seem convinced, and he grew very desperate. He felt he was not doing it at all properly, and he determined that he would spend next to nothing on his dinner. He remembered with a shudder the place he had taken the tramp to dinner, and he vowed that before he would economize as rigidly as that he would starve; but he had heard of the *table d'hôte* places on Sixth Avenue, so he went there and wandered along the street until he found one that looked clean and nice. He began with a heavy soup, shoved a rich, fat, fried fish over his plate, and followed it with a queer *entrée* of spaghetti with a tomato dressing that satisfied his hunger and killed his appetite as if with the blow of a lead pipe. But he went through with the rest of it, for he felt it was the truest economy to get his money's worth, and the limp salad in bad oil and the ice-cream of sour milk made him feel that eating was a positive pain rather than a pleasure; and in this state of mind and body, drugged and disgusted, he lighted his pipe and walked slowly towards the club along Twenty-sixth Street.

He looked in at the *café* at Delmonico's with envy and disgust, and, going disheartenedly on, passed the dining-room windows that were wide open and showed the heavy white linen, the silver, and the women coolly dressed and everybody happy.

And then there was a wild waving of arms inside, and white hands beckoning him, and he saw with mingled feelings of regret that the whole party of the Fourth of July were inside and motioning to him. They made room for him, and the captain's daughter helped him to olives, and the chaperon told how they had come into town for the day, and had been telegraphing for him and Edgar and Fred and "dear Bill," and the rest said they were so glad to see him because they knew he could appreciate a good dinner if any one could.

But Van Bibber only groaned, and the awful memories of the lead-like spaghetti and the bad oil and the queer cheese made him shudder, and turned things before him into a Tantalus feast of rare cruelty. There were Little Neck clams, delicious cold consommé, and white fish, and French chops with a dressing of truffles, and Roman punch and woodcock to follow, and crisp lettuce and toasted crackers-and-cheese, with a most remarkable combination of fruits and ices; and Van Bibber could eat nothing, and sat unhappily looking at his plate and shaking his head when the waiter urged him gently.

"Economy!" he said, with disgusted solemnity. "It's all tommy rot. It wouldn't have cost me a cent to have eaten this dinner, and yet I've paid half a dollar to make myself ill so that I can't. If you know how to economize, it may be all right; but if you don't understand it, you must leave it alone. It's dangerous. I'll economize no more."

And he accordingly broke his vow by taking the whole party up to see the lady who would not be photographed in tights, and put them in a box where they were gagged by the comedian, and where the soubrette smiled on them and all went well.

MR. TRAVERS'S FIRST HUNT

Young Travers, who had been engaged to a girl down on Long Island for the last three months, only met her father and brother a few weeks before the day set for the wedding. The brother is a master of hounds near Southampton, and shared the expense of importing a pack from England with Van Bibber. The father and son talked horse all day and until one in the morning; for they owned fast thoroughbreds, and entered them at the Sheepshead Bay and other race-tracks. Old Mr. Paddock, the father of the girl to whom Travers was engaged, had often said that when a young man asked him for his daughter's hand he would ask him in return, not if he had lived straight, but if he could ride straight. And on his answering this question in the affirmative depended his gaining her parent's consent. Travers had met Miss Paddock and her mother in Europe, while the men of the family were at home. He was invited to their place in the fall when the hunting season opened, and spent the evening most pleasantly and satisfactorily with his *fiancée* in a corner of the drawing-room. But as soon as the women had gone, young Paddock joined him and said, "You ride, of course?" Travers had never ridden; but he had been prompted how to answer by Miss Paddock, and so said there was nothing he liked better. As he expressed it, he would rather ride than sleep.

"That's good," said Paddock. "I'll give you a mount on Satan to-morrow morning at the meet. He is a bit nasty at the start of the season; and ever since he killed Wallis, the second groom, last year, none of us care much to ride him. But you can manage him, no doubt. He'll just carry your weight."

Mr. Travers dreamed that night of taking large, desperate leaps into space on a wild horse that snorted forth flames, and that rose at solid stone walls as though they were hayricks.

He was tempted to say he was ill in the morning—which was, considering his state of mind, more or less true—but concluded that, as he would have to ride sooner or later during his visit, and that if he did break his neck it would be in a good cause, determined to do his best. He did not want to ride at all, for two excellent reasons—first, because he wanted to live for Miss Paddock's sake, and, second, because he wanted to live for his own.

The next morning was a most forbidding and doleful-looking morning, and young Travers had great hopes that the meet would be declared off; but, just as he lay in doubt, the servant knocked at his door with his riding things and his hot water.

He came down-stairs looking very miserable indeed. Satan had been taken to the place where they were to meet, and Travers viewed him on his arrival there with a sickening sense of fear as he saw him pulling three grooms off their feet.

Travers decided that he would stay with his feet on solid earth just as long as he could, and when the hounds were thrown off and the rest had started at a gallop he waited, under the pretence of adjusting his gaiters, until they were all well away. Then he clenched his teeth, crammed his hat down over his ears, and scrambled up on to the saddle. His feet fell quite by accident into the stirrups, and the next instant he was off after the others, with an indistinct feeling that he was on a locomotive that was jumping the ties. Satan was in among and had passed the other horses in less than five minutes, and was so close on the hounds that the whippers-in gave a cry of warning. But Travers could as soon have pulled a boat back from going over the Niagara Falls as Satan, and it was only because the hounds were well ahead that saved them from having Satan ride them down. Travers had taken hold of the saddle with his left hand to keep himself down, and sawed and swayed on the reins with his right. He shut his eyes whenever Satan jumped, and never knew how he happened to stick on; but he did stick on, and was so far ahead that no one could see in the misty morning just how badly he rode. As it was, for daring and speed he led the field, and not even young Paddock was near him from the start. There was a broad stream in front of him, and a hill just on its other side. No one had ever tried to take this at a jump. It was considered more of a swim than anything else, and the hunters always crossed it by the bridge, towards the left. Travers saw the bridge and tried to jerk Satan's head in that direction; but Satan kept right on as straight as an express train over the prairie. Fences and trees and furrows passed by and under Travers like a panorama run by electricity, and he only breathed by accident. They went on at the stream and the hill beyond as though they were riding at a stretch of turf, and, though the whole field set up a shout of warning and dismay, Travers could only gasp and shut his eyes. He remembered the fate of the second groom and shivered. Then the horse rose like a rocket, lifting Travers so high in the air that he thought Satan would never come down again; but he did come down, with his feet bunched, on the opposite side of the stream. The next instant he was up and over the hill, and had stopped panting in the very centre of the pack that were snarling and snapping around the fox. And then Travers showed that he was a thoroughbred, even though he could not ride, for he hastily fumbled for his cigar-case, and when the field came pounding up over the bridge and around the hill, they saw him seated nonchalantly on his saddle, puffing critically at a cigar and giving Satan patronizing pats on the head.

"My dear girl," said old Mr. Paddock to his daughter as they rode back, "if you love that young man of yours and want to keep him, make him promise to give up riding. A more reckless and more brilliant horseman I have never seen. He took that double jump at the gate and that stream like a centaur. But he will break his neck sooner or later, and he ought to be stopped." Young Paddock was so delighted with his prospective brother-in-law's great riding that that night in the smoking-room he made him a present of Satan before all the men.

"No," said Travers, gloomily, "I can't take him. Your sister has asked me to give up what is dearer to me than anything next to herself, and that is my riding. You see, she is absurdly anxious for my safety, and she has asked me to promise never to ride again, and I have given my word."

A chorus of sympathetic remonstrance rose from the men.

"Yes, I know," said Travers to her brother, "it is rough, but it just shows what sacrifices a man will make for the woman he loves."

LOVE ME, LOVE MY DOG

Young Van Bibber had been staying with some people at Southampton, L.I., where, the fall before, his friend Travers made his reputation as a cross-country rider. He did this, it may be remembered, by shutting his eyes and holding on by the horse's mane and letting the horse go as it pleased. His recklessness and courage are still spoken of with awe; and the place where he cleared the water jump that every one else avoided is pointed out as Travers's Leap to visiting horsemen, who look at it gloomily and shake their heads. Miss Arnett, whose mother was giving the house-party, was an attractive young woman, with an admiring retinue of youths who gave attention without intention, and for none of whom Miss Arnett showed particular preference. Her whole interest, indeed, was centred in a dog, a Scotch collie called Duncan. She allowed this dog every liberty, and made a decided nuisance of him for every one around her. He always went with her when she walked, or trotted beside her horse when she rode. He stretched himself before the fire in the dining-room, and startled people at table by placing his cold nose against their hands or putting his paws on their gowns. He was generally voted a most annoying adjunct to the Arnett household; but no one dared hint so to Miss Arnett, as she only loved those who loved the dog, or pretended to do it. On the morning of the afternoon on which Van Bibber and his bag arrived, the dog disappeared and could not be recovered. Van Bibber found the household in a state of much excitement in consequence, and his welcome was necessarily brief. The arriving guest was not to be considered at all with the departed dog. The men told Van Bibber, in confidence, that the general relief among the guests was something ecstatic, but this was marred later by the gloom of Miss Arnett and her inability to think of anything else but the finding of the lost collie. Things became so feverish that for the sake of rest and peace the house-party proposed to contribute to a joint purse for the return of the dog, as even, nuisance as it was, it was not so bad as having their visit spoiled by Miss Arnett's abandonment to grief and crossness.

"I think," said the young woman, after luncheon, "that some of you men might be civil enough to offer to look for him. I'm sure he can't have gone far, or, if he has been stolen, the men who took him couldn't have gone very far away either. Now which of you will volunteer? I'm sure you'll do it to please me. Mr. Van Bibber, now: you say you're so clever. We're all the time hearing of your adventures. Why don't you show how full of expedients you are and rise to the occasion?" The suggestion of scorn in this speech nettled Van Bibber.

"I'm sure I never posed as being clever," he said, "and finding a lost dog with all Long Island to pick and choose from isn't a particularly easy thing to pull off successfully, I should think."

"I didn't suppose you'd take a dare like that, Van Bibber," said one of the men. "Why, it's just the sort of thing you do so well."

"Yes," said another, "I'll back you to find him if you try."

"Thanks," said Van Bibber, dryly. "There seems to be a disposition on the part of the young men present to turn me into a dog-catcher. I doubt whether this is altogether unselfish. I do not say that they would rather remain indoors and teach the girls how to play billiards, but I quite appreciate their reasons for not wishing to roam about in the snow and whistle for a dog. However, to oblige the despondent mistress of this valuable member of the household, I will risk pneumonia, and I will, at the same time, in order to make the event interesting to all concerned, back myself to bring that dog back by eight o'clock. Now, then, if any of you unselfish youths have any sporting blood, you will just name the sum."

They named one hundred dollars, and arranged that Van Bibber was to have the dog back by eight o'clock, or just in time for dinner; for Van Bibber said he wouldn't miss his dinner for all the dogs in the two hemispheres, unless the dogs happened to be his own.

Van Bibber put on his great-coat and told the man to bring around the dog-cart; then he filled his pockets with cigars and placed a flask of brandy under the seat, and wrapped the robes around his knees.

"I feel just like a relief expedition to the North Pole. I think I ought to have some lieutenants," he suggested.

"Well," cried one of the men, "suppose we make a pool and each chip in fifty dollars, and the man who brings the dog back in time gets the whole of it?"

"That bet of mine stands, doesn't it?" asked Van Bibber.

The men said it did, and went off to put on their riding things, and four horses were saddled and brought around from the stable. Each of the four explorers was furnished with a long rope to tie to Duncan's collar, and with which he was to be led back if they found him. They were cheered ironically by the maidens they had deserted on compulsion, and were smiled upon severally by Miss Arnett. Then they separated and took different roads. It was snowing gently, and was very cold. Van Bibber drove aimlessly ahead, looking to the right and left and scanning each back yard and side street. Every now and then he hailed some passing farm wagon and asked the driver if he had seen a stray collie dog, but the answer was invariably in the negative. He soon left the village in the rear, and plunged out over the downs. The wind was bitter cold, and swept from the water with a chill that cut through his clothes.

"Oh, this is great," said Van Bibber to the patient horse in front of him; "this *is* sport, this is. The next time I come to this part of the world I'll be dragged here with a rope. Nice, hospitable people those Arnetts, aren't they? Ask you to make yourself at home chasing dogs over an ice fjord. Don't know when I've enjoyed myself so much." Every now and then he stood up and looked all over the hills and valleys to see if he could not distinguish a black object running over the white surface of the snow, but he saw nothing like a dog, not even the track of one.

Twice he came across one of the other men, shivering and swearing from his saddle, and with teeth chattering.

"Well," said one of them, shuddering, "you haven't found that dog yet, I see."

"No," said Van Bibber. "Oh, no. I've given up looking for the dog. I'm just driving around enjoying myself. The air's so invigorating, and I like to feel the snow settling between my collar and the back of my neck."

At four o'clock Van Bibber was about as nearly frozen as a man could be after he had swallowed half a bottle of brandy. It was so cold that the ice formed on his cigar when he took it from his lips, and his feet and the dashboard seemed to have become stuck together.

"I think I'll give it up," he said, finally, as he turned the horse's head towards Southampton. "I hate to lose three hundred and fifty dollars as much as any man; but I love my fair young life, and I'm not going to turn into an equestrian statue in ice for anybody's collie dog."

He drove the cart to the stable and unharnessed the horse himself, as all the grooms were out scouring the country, and then went upstairs unobserved and locked himself in his room, for he did not care to have the others know that he had given out so early in the chase. There was a big open fire in his room, and he put on his warm things and stretched out before it in a great easy-chair, and smoked and sipped the brandy and chuckled with delight as he thought of the four other men racing around in the snow.

"They may have more nerve than I," he soliloquized, "and I don't say they have not; but they can have all the credit and rewards they want, and I'll be satisfied to stay just where I am."

At seven he saw the four riders coming back dejectedly, and without the dog. As they passed his room he heard one of the men ask if Van Bibber had got back yet, and another say yes, he had, as he had left the cart in the stable, but that one of the servants had said that he had started out again on foot.

"He has, has he?" said the voice. "Well, he's got sporting blood, and he'll need to keep it at fever heat if he expects to live. I'm frozen so that I can't bend my fingers."

Van Bibber smiled, and moved comfortably in the big chair; he had dozed a little, and was feeling very contented. At half-past seven he began to dress, and at five minutes to eight he was ready for dinner and stood looking out of the window at the moonlight on the white lawn below. The snow had stopped falling, and everything lay quiet and still as though it were cut in marble. And then suddenly, across the lawn, came a black, bedraggled object on four legs, limping painfully, and lifting its feet as though there were lead on them.

"Great heavens!" cried Van Bibber, "it's the dog!" He was out of the room in a moment and down into the hall. He heard the murmur of voices in the drawing-room, and the sympathetic tones of the women who were pitying the men. Van Bibber pulled on his overshoes and a great-coat that covered him from his ears to his ankles, and dashed out into the snow. The dog had just enough spirit left to try and dodge him, and with a leap to one side went off again across the lawn. It was, as Van Bibber knew, but three minutes to eight o'clock, and have the dog he must and would. The collie sprang first to one side and then to the other, and snarled and snapped; but Van Bibber was keen with the excitement of the chase, so he plunged forward recklessly and tackled the dog around the body, and they both rolled over and over together. Then Van Bibber scrambled to his feet and dashed up the steps and into the drawing-room just as the people were in line for dinner, and while the minute-hand stood at a minute to eight o'clock.

"How is this?" shouted Van Bibber, holding up one hand and clasping the dog under his other arm.

Miss Arnett flew at the collie and embraced it, wet as it was, and ruined her gown, and all the men glanced instinctively at the clock and said:

"You've won, Van."

"But you must be frozen to death," said Miss Arnett, looking up at him with gratitude in her eyes.

"Yes, yes," said Van Bibber, beginning to shiver. "I've had a terrible long walk, and I had to carry him all the way. If you'll excuse me, I'll go change my things."

He reappeared again in a suspiciously short time for one who had to change outright, and the men admired his endurance and paid up the bet.

"Where did you find him, Van?" one of them asked.

"Oh, yes," they all chorused. "Where was he?"

"That," said Mr. Van Bibber, "is a thing known to only two beings, Duncan and myself. Duncan can't tell, and I won't. If I did, you'd say I was trying to make myself out clever, and I never boast about the things I do."

ELEANORE CUYLER

Miss Eleanore Cuyler had dined alone with her mother that night, and she was now sitting in the drawing-room, near the open fire, with her gloves and fan on the divan beside her, for she was going out later to a dance.

She was reading a somewhat weighty German review, and the contrast which the smartness of her gown presented to the seriousness of her occupation made her smile slightly as she paused for a moment to cut the leaves.

And when the bell sounded in the hall she put the book away from her altogether, and wondered who it might be.

It might be young Wainwright, with the proof-sheets of the new story he had promised to let her see, or flowers for the dance from Bruce-Brice, of the English Legation at Washington, who for the time being was practising diplomatic moves in New York, or some of her working-girls with a new perplexity for her to unravel, or only one of the men from the stable to tell her how her hunter was getting on after his fall. It might be any of these and more. The possibilities were diverse and all of interest, and she acknowledged this to herself, with a little sigh of content that it was so. For she found her pleasure in doing many things, and in the fact that there were so many. She rejoiced daily that she was free, and her own mistress in everything; free to do these many things denied to other young women, and that she had the health and position and cleverness to carry them on and through to success. She did them all, and equally well and gracefully, whether it was the rejection of a too ambitious devotee who dared to want to have her all to himself, or the planning of a woman's luncheon, or the pushing of a bill to provide kindergartens in the public schools. But it was rather a relief when the man opened the curtains and said, "Mr. Wainwright," and Wainwright walked quickly towards her, tugging at his glove.

"You are very good to see me so late," he said, speaking as he entered, "but I had to see you to-night, and I wasn't asked to that dance. I'm going away," he went on, taking his place by the fire, with his arm resting on the mantel. He had a trick of standing there when he had something of interest to say, and he was tall and well-looking enough to appear best in that position, and she was used to it. He was the most frequent of her visitors.

"Going away," she repeated, smiling up at him; "not for long, I hope. Where are you going now?"

"I'm going to London," he said. "They cabled me this morning. It seems they've taken the play, and are going to put it on at once." He smiled, and blushed slightly at her exclamation of pleasure. "Yes, it is rather nice. It seems

'Jilted' was a failure, and they've taken it off, and are going to put on 'School,' with the old cast, until they can get my play rehearsed, and they want me to come over and suggest things."

She stopped him with another little cry of delight that was very sweet to him, and full of moment.

"Oh, how glad I am!" she said. "How proud you must be! Now, why do you pretend you are not? And I suppose Tree and the rest of them will be in the cast, and all that dreadful American colony in the stalls, and you will make a speech—and I won't be there to hear it." She rose suddenly with a quick, graceful movement, and held out her hand to him, which he took, laughing and conscious-looking with pleasure.

She sank back on the divan, and shook her head doubtfully at him. "When will you stop?" she said. "Don't tell me you mean to be an Admirable Crichton. You are too fine for that."

He looked down at the fire, and said, slowly, "It is not as if I were trying my hand at an entirely different kind of work. No, I don't think I did wrong in dramatizing it. The papers all said, when the book first came out, that it would make a good play; and then so many men wrote to me for permission to dramatize it that I thought I might as well try to do it myself. No, I think it is in line with my other work. I don't think I am straying after strange gods."

"You should not," she said, softly. "The old ones have been so kind to you. But you took me too seriously," she added.

"I am afraid sometimes," he answered, "that you do not know how seriously I do take you."

"Yes, I do," she said, quickly. "And when I am serious, that is all very well; but to-night I only want to laugh. I am very happy, it is such good news. And after the New York managers refusing it, too. They will *have* to take it *now*, now that it is a London success."

"Well, it isn't a London success yet," he said, dryly. "The books went well over there because the kind of Western things I wrote about met their ideas of this country—cowboys and prairies and Indian maidens and all that. And so I rather hope the play will suit them for the same reason."

"And you will go out a great deal, I hope," she said. "Oh, you will have to! You will find so many people to like, almost friends already. They were talking about you even when I was there, and I used to shine in reflected glory because I knew you."

"Yes, I can fancy it," he said. "But I should like to see something of them if I have time. Lowes wants me to stay with them, and I suppose I will. He would feel hurt if I didn't. He has a most absurd idea of what I did for him on the ranche when he had the fever that time, and ever since he went back to enjoy his ill-gotten gains and his title and all that, he has kept writing to me to come out. Yes, I suppose I will stay with them. They are in town now."

Miss Cuyler's face was still lit with pleasure at his good fortune, but her smile was less spontaneous than it had been. "That will be very nice. I quite envy you," she said. "I suppose you know about his sister?"

"The Honorable Evelyn?" he asked. "Yes; he used to have a photograph of her, and I saw some others the other day in a shop-window on Broadway."

"She is a very nice girl," Miss Cuyler said, thoughtfully. "I wonder how you two will get along?" and then she added, as if with sudden compunction, "but I am sure you will like her very much. She is very clever, besides."

"I don't know how a professional beauty will wear if one sees her every day at breakfast," he said. "One always associates them with functions and varnishing days and lawn-parties. You will write to me, will you not?" he added.

"That sounds," she said, "as though you meant to be gone such a very long time."

He turned one of the ornaments on the mantel with his fingers, and looked at it curiously. "It depends," he said, slowly—"it depends on so many things. No," he went on, looking at her; "it does not depend on many things; just on one."

Miss Cuyler looked up at him questioningly, and then down again very quickly, and reached meaninglessly for the book beside her. She saw something in his face and in the rigidity of his position that made her breathe more rapidly. She had not been afraid of this from him, because she had always taken the attitude towards him of a very dear friend and of one who was older, not in years, but in experience of the world, for she had lived abroad while he had gone from the university to the West, which he had made his own, in books. They were both very young.

She did not want him to say anything. She could only answer him in one way, and in a way that would hurt and give pain to them both. She had hoped he could remain just as he was, a very dear friend, with a suggestion sometimes in the background of his becoming something more. She was, of course, too experienced to believe in a long platonic friendship.

Uppermost in her mind was the thought that, no matter what he urged, she must remember that she wanted to be free, to live her own life, to fill her own sphere of usefulness, and she must not let him tempt her to forget this. She had next to consider him, and that she must be hard and keep him from speaking at all; and this was very difficult, for she cared for him very dearly. She strengthened her determination by thinking of his going away, and of how glad she would be when he had gone that she had committed herself to nothing. This absence would be a test for both of them; it could not have been better had it been arranged on purpose. She had ideas of what she could best do for those around her, and she must not be controlled and curbed, no matter how strongly she might think she wished it. She must not give way to the temptation of the moment, or to a passing mood. And then there were other men. She had their photographs on her dressing-table, and liked each for some qualities the others did not possess in such a degree; but she liked them all because no one of them had the right to say "must" or even "you might" to her, and she fancied that the moment she gave one of them this right she would hate him cordially, and would fly to the others for sympathy; and she was not a young woman who thought that matrimony meant freedom to fly to any one but her husband for that. But this one of the men was a little the worst; he made it harder for her to be quite herself. She noticed that when she was with him she talked more about her feelings than with the other men, with whom she was satisfied to discuss the play, or what girl they wanted to take into dinner. She had touches of remorse after these confidences to Wainwright, and wrote him brisk, friendly notes the next morning, in which the words "your friend" were always sure to appear, either markedly at the beginning or at the end, or tucked away in the middle. She thought by this to unravel the web she might have woven the day before. But she had apparently failed. She stood up suddenly from pure nervousness, and crossed the room as though she meant to go to the piano, which was a very unfortunate move, as she seldom played, and never for him. She sat down before it, nevertheless, rather hopelessly, and crossed her hands in front of her. He had turned, and followed her with his eyes; they were very bright and eager, and her own faltered as she looked at them.

"You do not show much interest in the one thing that will bring me back," he said. He spoke reproachfully and yet a little haughtily, as though he had already half suspected she had guessed what he meant to say.

"Ah, you cannot tell how long you will be there," she said, lightly. "You will like it much more than you think. I—" she stopped hopelessly, and glanced, without meaning to do so, at the clock-face on the mantel beside him.

"Oh," he said, with quick misunderstanding, "I beg your pardon, I am keeping you, I forgot how late it was, and you are going out." He came towards her as though he meant to go. She stood up and made a quick, impatient gesture with her hands. He was making it very hard for her.

"Fancy!" she said. "You know I want to talk to you; what does the dance matter? Why are you so unlike yourself?" she went on, gently. "And it is our last night, too."

The tone of her words seemed to reassure him, for he came nearer and rested his elbow beside her on the piano and said, "Then you are sorry that I am going?"

It was very hard to be unyielding to him when he spoke and looked as he did then; but she repeated to herself, "He will be gone to-morrow, and then I shall be so thankful that I did not bind myself—that I am still free. He will be gone, and I shall be so glad. It will only be a minute now before he goes, and if I am strong I will rejoice at leisure." So she looked up at him without a sign of the effort it cost her, frankly and openly, and said, "Sorry? Of course I am sorry. One does not have so many friends that one can spare them for long, even to have them grow famous. I think it is very selfish of you to go, for you are famous enough already."

As he looked at her and heard her words running on smoothly and meaninglessly, he knew that it was quite useless to speak, and he grew suddenly colder, and sick, and furious at once with a confused anger and bitterness. And then, for he was quite young, so young that he thought it was the manly thing to do to carry his grief off lightly instead of rather being proud of his love, however she might hold it,—he drew himself up and began pulling carefully at his glove.

"Yes," he said, slowly, "I fancy the change will be very pleasant." He was not thinking of his words or of how thoughtless they must sound. He was only anxious to get away without showing how deeply he was hurt. If he had not done this; if he had let her see how miserable he was, and that plays and books and such things were nothing to him now, and that she was just all there was in the whole world to him, it might have ended differently. But he was untried, and young. So he buttoned the left glove with careful scrutiny and said, "They always start those boats at such absurd hours; the tides never seem to suit one; you have to go on board without breakfast, or else stay on board the night before, and that's so unpleasant. Well, I hope you will enjoy the dance, and tell them I was very much hurt that I wasn't asked."

He held out his hand quite steadily. "I will write you if you will let me," he went on, "and send you word where I am as soon as I know." She took his hand and said, "Good-by, and I hope it will be a grand success: I know it will. And come back soon; and, yes, do write to me. I hope you will have a very pleasant voyage."

He had reached the door and stopped uncertainly at the curtains. "Thank you," he said; and "Oh," he added, politely, "will you say good-by to your mother for me, please?"

She nodded her head and smiled and said, "Yes; I will not forget. Good-by."

She did not move until she heard the door close upon him, and then she turned towards the window as though she could still follow him through the closed blinds, and then she walked over to the divan and picked up her fan and gloves and remained looking down at them in her hand. The room seemed very empty. She glanced at the place where he had stood and at the darkened windows again, and sank down very slowly against the cushions of the divan, and pressed her hands against her cheeks.

She did not hear the rustle of her mother's dress as she came down the stairs and parted the curtains.

"Are you ready, Eleanore?" she said, briskly. "Tell me, how does this lace look? I think there is entirely too much of it."

It was a month after this, simultaneously with the announcements by cable of the instant success in London of "A Western Idyl," that Miss Cuyler retired from the world she knew, and disappeared into darkest New York by the way of Rivington Street. She had discovered one morning that she was not ill nor run down nor overtaxed, but just mentally tired of all things, and that what she needed was change of air and environment, and unselfish work for the good of others, and less thought of herself. Her mother's physician suggested to her, after a secret and hasty interview with Mrs. Cuyler, that change of air was good, but that the air of Rivington Street was not of the best; and her friends, both men and women, assured her that they appreciated her much more than the people of the east side possibly could do, and that they were much more worthy of her consideration, and in a fair way of improvement yet if she would only continue to shine upon and before them. But she was determined in her purpose, and regarded the College Settlement as the one opening and refuge for the energies which had too long been given to the arrangement of paper chases across country, and the routine of society, and dilettante interest in kindergartens. Life had become for her real and earnest, and she rejected Bruce-Brice of the British Legation with the sad and hopeless kindness of one who almost contemplates taking the veil, and to whom the things of this world outside of tenements are hollow and unprofitable. She found a cruel disappointment at first, for the women of the College Settlement had rules and ideas of their own, and had seen enthusiasts like herself come into Rivington Street before, and depart again. She had thought she would nurse the sick and visit the prisoners on the Island, and bring cleanliness and hope into miserable lives, but she found that this was the work of women tried in the service, who understood it, and who made her first serve her apprenticeship by reading the German Bible to old women whose eyes were dim, but who were as hopelessly clean and quite as self-respecting in their way as herself. The heroism and the self-sacrifice of a Father Damien or a Florence Nightingale were not for her; older and wiser young women saw to that work with a quiet matter-of-fact cheerfulness and a common-sense that bewildered her. And they treated her kindly, but indulgently, as an outsider. It took her some time to understand this, and she did not confess to herself without a struggle that she was disappointed in her own usefulness; but she brought herself to confess it to her friends "uptown," when she visited that delightful country from which she was self-exiled. She went there occasionally for an afternoon's rest or to a luncheon or a particularly attractive dinner, but she always returned to the Settlement at night, and this threw an additional interest about her to her friends—an interest of which she was ashamed, for she knew how little she was really doing, and that her sacrifice was one of discomfort merely. The good she did now, it was humiliating to acknowledge, was in no way proportionate to that which her influence had wrought among people of her own class.

And what made it very hard was that wherever she went they seemed to talk of him. Now it would be a girl just from the other side who had met him on the terrace of the Lower House, "where he seemed to know every one," and another had driven with him to Ascot, where he had held the reins, and had shown them what a man who had guided a mail-coach one whole winter over the mountains for a living could do with a coach for pleasure. And many of the men had met him at the clubs and at house parties in the country, and they declared with enthusiastic envy that he was no end of a success. Her English friends all wrote of him, and wanted to know all manner of little things concerning him, and hinted that they understood they were very great friends. The papers seemed to be always having him doing something, and there was apparently no one else in London who could so properly respond to the toasts of America at all the public dinners. She had had letters from him herself—of course bright, clever ones—that suggested what a wonderfully full and happy life his was, but with no reference to his return. He was living with his young friend Lord Lowes, and went everywhere with him and his people; and then as a final touch, which she had already anticipated, people began to speak of him and the Honorable Evelyn. What could be more natural? they said. He had saved her brother's life while out West half a dozen times at least, from all accounts; and he was rich, and well-looking, and well-born, and rapidly becoming famous.

A young married woman announced it at a girls' luncheon. She had it from her friend the Marchioness of Pelby, who was Evelyn's first-cousin. So far, only the family had been told; but all London knew it, and it was said that Lord Lowes was very much pleased. One of the girls at the table said you never could tell about those things; she had no doubt the Marchioness of Pelby was an authority, but she would wait until she got their wedding-cards before she believed it. For some reason this girl did not look at Miss Cuyler, and Miss Cuyler felt grateful to her, and thought she was a nice, bright little thing; and then another girl said it was only turn about. The Englishmen had taken all the attractive American girls, and it was only fair that the English girls should get some of the nice American men. This girl was an old friend of Eleanore's; but she was surprised at her making such a speech, and wondered why she had not noticed in her before similar exhibitions of bad taste. She walked back to Rivington Street from the luncheon; composing the letter she would write to him, congratulating him on his engagement. She composed several. Some of them were very short and cheery, and others rather longer and full of reminiscences. She wondered with sudden fierce bitterness how he could so soon forget certain walks and afternoons they had spent together; and the last note, which she composed in bed, was a very sad and scornful one, and so pathetic as a work of composition that she cried a little over it, and went to sleep full of indignation that she had cried.

She told herself the next morning that she had cried because she was frankly sorry to lose the companionship of so old and good a friend, and because now that she had been given much more important work to do, she was naturally saddened by the life she saw around her, and weakened by the foul air of the courts and streets, and the dreary environments of the tenements. As for him, she was happy in his happiness; and she pictured how some day, when he proudly brought his young bride to this country to show her to his friends, he would ask after her. And they would say: "Who! Eleanore Cuyler? Why, don't you know? While you were on your honeymoon she was in the slums, where she took typhoid fever nursing a child, and died!" Or else some day, when she had grown into a beautiful sweet-faced old lady, with white hair, his wife would die, and he would return to her, never having been very happy with his first wife, but having nobly hidden from her and from the world his true feelings. He would find her working among the poor, and would ask her forgiveness, and she could not quite determine whether she would forgive him or not. These pictures comforted her even while they saddened her, and she went about her work, feeling that it was now her life's work, and that she was in reality an old, old woman. The rest, she was sure, was but a weary waiting for the end.

It was about six months after this, in the early spring, while Miss Cuyler was still in Rivington Street, that young Van Bibber invited his friend Travers to dine with him, and go on later to the People's Theatre, on the Bowery, where

Irving Willis, the Boy Actor, was playing "Nick of the Woods." Travers despatched a hasty and joyous note in reply to this to the effect that he would be on hand. He then went off with a man to try a horse at a riding academy, and easily and promptly forgot all about it. He did remember, as he was dressing for dinner, that he had an appointment somewhere, and took some consolation out of this fact, for he considered it a decided step in advance when he could remember that he had an engagement, even if he could not recall what it was. The stern mental discipline necessary to do this latter would, he hoped, come in time. So he dined unwarily at home, and was, in consequence, seized upon by his father, who sent him to the opera, as a substitute for himself, with his mother and sisters, while he went off delightedly to his club to play whist.

Travers did not care for the opera, and sat in the back of the box and dozed, and wondered moodily what so many nice men saw in his sisters to make them want to talk to them. It was midnight, and just as he had tumbled into bed, when the nature of his original engagement came back to him, and his anger and disappointment were so intense that he kicked the clothes over the foot of his bedstead.

As for Van Bibber, he knew his friend too well to wait for him, and occupied a box at the People's Theatre in solitary state, and from its depths gurgled with delight whenever the Boy Actor escaped being run over by a real locomotive, or in turn rescued the stout heroine from six red shirted cowboys. There were quite as many sudden deaths and lofty sentiments as he had expected, and he left the theatre with the pleased satisfaction of an evening well spent and with a pitying sympathy for Travers who had missed it. The night was pleasant and filled with the softness of early spring, and Van Bibber turned down the Bowery with a cigar between his teeth and no determined purpose except the one that he did not intend to go to bed. The streets were still crowded, and the lights showed the many types of this "Thieves' Highway" with which Van Bibber, in his many excursions in search of mild adventure, had become familiar. They were so familiar that the unfamiliarity of the hurrying figure of a girl of his own class who passed in front of him down Grand Street brought him, abruptly wondering, to a halt. She had passed directly under an electric light, and her dress, and walk, and bearing he seemed to recognize, but as belonging to another place. What a girl, well-born and well-dressed, could be doing at such an hour in such a neighborhood aroused his curiosity; but it was rather with a feeling of *noblesse oblige*, and a hope of being of use to one of his own people, that he crossed to the opposite side of the street and followed her. She was evidently going somewhere; that was written in every movement of her regular quick walk and her steadfast look ahead. Her veil hid the upper part of her face, and the passing crowd shut her sometimes entirely from view; but Van Bibber, himself unnoticed, succeeded in keeping her in sight, while he speculated as to the nature of her errand and her personality. At Eldridge Street she turned sharply to the north, and, without a change in her hurrying gait, passed on quickly, and turned again at Rivington. "Oh," said Van Bibber, with relieved curiosity, "one of the College Settlement," and stopped satisfied. But the street had now become deserted, and though he disliked the idea of following a woman, even though she might not be aware of his doing so, he disliked even more the idea of leaving her to make her way in such a place alone. And so he started on again, and as there was now more likelihood of her seeing him in the empty street, he dropped farther to the rear and kept in the shadow; and as he did so, he saw a man, whom he had before noticed on the opposite side of the street, quicken his pace and draw nearer to the girl. It seemed impossible to Van Bibber that any man could mistake the standing of this woman and the evident purpose of her haste; but the man was apparently settling his pace to match hers, as if only waiting an opportunity to approach her. Van Bibber tucked his stick under his arm and moved forward more quickly. It was midnight, and the street was utterly strange to him. From the light of the lamps he could see signs in Hebrew and the double eagle of Russia painted on the windows of the saloons. Long rows of trucks and drays stood ranged along the pavements for the night, and on some of the stoops and fire-escapes of the tenements a few dwarfish specimens of the Polish Jew sat squabbling in their native tongue.

But it was not until they had reached Orchard Street, and when Rivington Street was quite empty, that the man drew up uncertainly beside the girl, and, bending over, stared up in her face, and then, walking on at her side, surveyed her deliberately from head to foot. For a few steps the girl moved on as apparently unmindful of his near presence as though he were a stray dog running at her side; but when he stepped directly in front of her, she stopped and backed away from him fearfully. The man hesitated for an instant, and then came on after her, laughing.

Van Bibber had been some distance in the rear. He reached the curb beside them just as the girl turned back, with the man still following her, and stepped in between them. He had come so suddenly from out of the darkness that they both started. Van Bibber did not look at the man. He turned to the girl, and raised his hat slightly, and recognized Eleanore Cuyler instantly as he did so; but as she did not seem to remember him he did not call her by name, but simply said, with a jerk of his head, "Is this man annoying you?"

Miss Cuyler seemed to wish before everything else to avoid a scene.

"He—he just spoke to me, that is all," she said. "I live only a block below here; if you will please let me go on alone, I would be very much obliged."

"Certainly, do go on," said Van Bibber, "but I shall have to follow you until you get in-doors. You needn't be alarmed, no one will speak to you." Then he turned to the man, and said, in a lower tone, "You wait here till I get back, will you? I want to talk to you."

The man paid no attention to him whatsoever. He was so far misled by Van Bibber's appearance as to misunderstand the situation entirely. "Oh, come now," he said, smiling knowingly at the girl, "you can't shake me for no dude."

He put out his hand as he spoke as though he meant to touch her. Van Bibber pulled his stick from under his arm and tossed it out of his way, and struck the man twice heavily in the face. He was very cool and determined about it, and punished him, in consequence, much more effectively than if his indignation had made him excited. The man gave a howl of pain, and stumbled backwards over one of the stoops, where he dropped moaning and swearing, with his fingers pressed against his face.

"*Please*, now," begged Van Bibber, quickly turning to Miss Cuyler, "I am very sorry, but if you had *only* gone when I asked you to." He motioned impatiently with his hand. "Will you please go?"

But the girl, to his surprise, stood still and looked past him over his shoulder. Van Bibber motioned again for her to pass on, and then, as she still hesitated, turned and glanced behind him. The street had the blue-black look of a New York street at night. There was not a lighted window in the block. It seemed to have grown suddenly more silent and dirty and desolate-looking. He could see the glow of the elevated station at Allen Street, and it seemed fully a half-mile away. Save for the girl and the groaning fool on the stoop, and the three figures closing in on him, he was quite alone. The foremost of the three men stopped running, and came up briskly with his finger held interrogatively in front of him. He stopped when it was within a foot of Van Bibber's face.

"Are you looking for a fight?" he asked.

There was enough of the element of the sport in Van Bibber to enable him to recognize the same element in the young man before him. He knew that this was no whimpering blackguard who followed women into side streets to insult them; this was one of the purest specimens of the tough of the East-Side water-front, and he and his companions would fight as readily as Van Bibber would smoke—and they would not fight fair. The adventure had taken on a grim and serious turn, and Van Bibber gave an imperceptible shrug and a barely audible exclamation of disgust as he accepted it.

"Because," continued his new opponent with business-like briskness, "if you're looking for a fight, you can set right to me. You needn't think you can come down here and run things—you—" He followed this with an easy roll of oaths, intended to goad his victim into action.

A reformed prize-fighter had once told Van Bibber that there were six rules to observe in a street fight. He said he had forgotten the first five, but the sixth one was to strike first. Van Bibber turned his head towards Miss Cuyler. "You had better run," he said, over his shoulder; and then, turning quickly, he brought his left fist, with all the strength and weight of his arm and body back of it, against the end of the new-comer's chin.

This is a most effective blow. This is so because the lower jaw is anatomically loose; and when it is struck heavily, it turns and jars the brain, and the man who is struck feels as though the man who struck him had opened the top of his skull and taken his brains in his hand and wrenched them as a brakeman wrenches a brake. If you shut your teeth hard, and rap the tip of your chin sharply with your knuckles, you can get an idea of how effective this is when multiplied by an arm and all the muscles of a shoulder.

The man threw up his arms and went over backwards, groping blindly with his hands.

Van Bibber heard a sharp rapping behind him frequently repeated; he could not turn to see what it was, for one of the remaining men was engaging him in front, and the other was kicking at his knee-cap, and striking at his head from behind. He was no longer cool; he was grandly and viciously excited; and, rushing past his opponent, he caught him over his hip with his left arm across his breast, and so tossed him, using his hip for a lever.

A man in this position can be thrown so that he will either fall as lightly as a baby falls from his pillow to the bed, or with sufficient force to break his ribs. Van Bibber, being excited, threw him the latter way. Seeing this, the second man, who had so far failed to find Van Bibber's knee-cap, backed rapidly away, with his hands in front of him.

"Here," he cried, "lem'me alone; I'm not in this."

"Oh yes, you are," cried Van Bibber, gasping, but with fierce politeness. "Excuse me, but you are. Put up your hands; I'm going to kill *you*."

He had a throbbing feeling in the back of his head, and his breathing was difficult. He could still hear the heavy, irregular rapping behind him, but it had become confused with the throbbing in his head. "Put up your hands," he panted.

The third man, still backing away, placed his arms in a position of defence, and Van Bibber beat them down savagely, and caught him by the throat and pounded him until his arm was tired, and he had to drop him at his feet.

As he turned dizzily, he heard a sharp answering rap down the street, and saw coming towards him the burly figure of a policeman running heavily and throwing his night-stick in front of him by its leather thong, so that it struck reverberating echoes out of the pavement.

And then he saw to his amazement that Miss Cuyler was still with him, standing by the curb and beating it with his heavy walking-stick as calmly as though she were playing golf, and looking keenly up and down the street for possible aid. Van Bibber gazed at her with breathless admiration.

"Good heavens!" he panted, "didn't I ask you *please* to go home?"

The policeman passed them and dived uncertainly down a dark area-way as one departing figure disappeared into the open doorway of a tenement, on his way to the roof, and the legs of another dodged between the line of drays.

"Where'd them fellows go?" gasped the officer, instantly reappearing up the steps of the basement.

"How should I know?" answered Van Bibber, and added, with ill-timed lightness, "they didn't leave any address." The officer stared at him with severe suspicion, and then disappeared again under one of the trucks.

"I am very, very much obliged to you, Miss Cuyler," Van Bibber said. He tried to raise his hat, but the efforts of the gentleman who had struck him from behind had been successful and the hat came off only after a wrench that made him wince.

"You were very brave," he went on. "And it was very good of you to stand by me. You won't mind my saying so, now, will you? But you gave the wrong rap. I hadn't time to tell you to change it." He mopped the back of his head tenderly with his handkerchief, and tried to smile cheerfully. "You see, you were giving the rap," he explained politely, "for a fire-engine; but it's of no consequence." Miss Cuyler came closer to him, and he saw that her face showed sudden anxiety.

"Mr. Van Bibber!" she exclaimed. "Oh, I didn't know it was you! I didn't know it was any one who knew me. What will you think?"

"I beg your pardon," said Van Bibber, blankly.

"You must not believe," she went on, quickly, "that I am subject to this sort of thing. Please do not imagine I am annoyed down here like this. It has never happened before. I was nursing a woman, and her son, who generally goes home with me, was kept at the works, and I thought I could risk getting back alone. You see," she explained, as Van Bibber's face showed he was still puzzled, "my people do not fancy my living down here; and if they should hear of this they would never consent to my remaining another day, and it means so much to me now."

"They need not hear of it," Van Bibber answered, sympathetically. "They certainly won't from me, if that's what you mean."

The officer had returned, and interrupted them brusquely. It seemed to him that he was not receiving proper attention.

"Say, what's wrong here?" he demanded. "Did that gang take anything off'n you."

"They did not," said Van Bibber. "They held me up, but they didn't take nothin' off'n of me."

The officer flushed uncomfortably, and was certain now that he was being undervalued. He surveyed the blood running down over Van Bibber's collar with a smile of malicious satisfaction.

"They done you up, any way," he suggested.

"Yes, they done me up," assented Van Bibber, cheerfully, "and if you'd come a little sooner they'd done you up too."

He stepped to Miss Cuyler's side, and they walked on down the street to the College Settlement in silence, the policeman following uncertainly in the rear.

"I haven't thanked you, Mr. Van Bibber," said Miss Cuyler. "It was really fine of you, and most exciting. You must be very strong. I can't imagine how you happened to be there, but it was most fortunate for me that you were. If you had not, I—"

"Oh, that's all right," said Van Bibber, hurriedly. "I haven't had so much fun without paying for it for a long time. Fun," he added, meditatively, "costs so much."

"And you will be so good, then, as not to speak of it," she said, as she gave him her hand at the door.

"Of course not. Why should I?" said Van Bibber, and then his face beamed and clouded again instantly. "But, oh," he begged, "I'm afraid I'll have to tell Travers! Oh, please let me tell Travers! I'll make him promise not to mention it, but it's too good a joke on him, when you think what he missed. You see," he added, hastily, "we were to have gone out together, and he forgot, as usual, and missed the whole thing, and he wasn't *in it*, and it will just about break his heart. He's always getting grinds on me," he went on, persuasively, "and now I've got this on him. You will really have to let me tell Travers."

Miss Cuyler looked puzzled and said "Certainly," though she failed to see why Mr. Travers should want his head broken, and then she thanked Van Bibber again and nodded to the officer and went in-doors.

The policeman, who had listened to the closing speeches, looked at Van Bibber with dawning admiration.

"Now then, officer," said Van Bibber, briskly, "which of the saloons around here break the law by keeping open after one? You probably know, and if you don't I'll have to take your number." And peace being in this way restored, the two disappeared together into the darkness to break the law.

Van Bibber told Travers about it the next morning, and Travers forgot he was not to mention it, and told the next man he met. By one o'clock the story had grown in his telling, and Van Bibber's reputation had grown with it.

Travers found three men breakfasting together at the club, and drew up a chair. "Have you heard the joke Van Bibber's got on me?" he asked, sadly, by way of introduction.

Wainwright was sitting at the next table with his back to them. He had just left the customs officers, and his wonder at the dirtiness of the streets and height of the buildings had given way to the pleasure of being home again, and before the knowledge that "old friends are best." He had meant to return again immediately as soon as he had arranged for the production of his play in New York; his second play was to be brought out in London in a month. But the heartiness of his friends' greetings, and the anxiety of men to be recognized who had been mere acquaintances hitherto, had touched and amused him. He was too young to be cynical over it, and he was glad, on the whole, that he had come back.

His mind was wide awake, and shifting from one pleasant thought to another, when he heard Travers's voice behind him raised impressively. "And they both went at Van hammer and tongs," he heard Travers say, "one in front and the other behind, kicking and striking all over the shop. And," continued Travers, interrupting himself suddenly with a shrill and anxious tone of interrogation, "where was I while this was going on? That's the pathetic part of it—where was I?" His voice rose to almost a shriek of disappointment. "*I* was sitting in a red-silk box listening to a red-silk opera with a lot of *girls*— that's what *I* was doing. I wasn't in it; I wasn't. I—"

"Well, never mind what you were doing," said one of the men, soothingly; "you weren't in it, as you say. Return to the libretto."

"Well," continued Travers, meekly, "let me see; where was I?"

"You were in a red-silk box," suggested one of the men, reaching for the coffee.

"Go on, Travers," said the first man. "The two men were kicking Van Bibber."

"Oh, yes," cried Travers. "Well, Van just threw the first fellow over his head, and threw him *hard*. He must have broken his ribs, for the second fellow tried to get away, and begged off, but Van wouldn't have it, and rushed him. He got the tough's head under his arm, and pummelled it till his arm ached, and then he threw him into the street, and asked if any other gentleman would like to try his luck. That's what Van did, and he told me not to tell any one, so I hope you will not mention it. But I had to tell you, because I want to know if you have ever met a harder case of hard luck than that. Think of it, will you? Think of me sitting there in a red-silk box listening to a—"

"What did the girl do?" interrupted one of the men.

"Oh, yes," said Travers, hastily; "that's the best part of it; that's the plot—the girl. Now, who do you think the girl was?" He looked around the table proudly, with the air of a man who is sure of his climax.

"How should I know?" one man said. "Some actress going home from the theatre, maybe—"

"No," said Travers. "It's a girl you all know." He paused impressively. "What would you say now," he went on, dropping his voice, "if I was to tell you it was Eleanore Cuyler?"

The three men looked up suddenly and at each other with serious concern. There was a moment's silence. "Well," said one of them, softly, "that *is* rather nasty."

"Now, what I want to know is," Travers ran on, elated at the sensation his narrative had made—"what I want to know is, where is that girl's mother, or sister, or brother? Have they anything to say? Has any one anything to say? Why, one of Eleanore Cuyler's little fingers is worth more than all the East and West Side put together; and she is to be allowed to run risks like—"

Wainwright pushed his chair back, and walked out of the room.

"See that fellow, quick," said Travers; "that's Wainwright who writes plays and things. He's a thoroughbred sport, too, and he just got back from London. It's in the afternoon papers."

Miss Cuyler was reading to Mrs. Lockmuller, who was old and bedridden and cross. Under the influence of Eleanore's low voice she frequently went to sleep, only to wake and demand ungratefully why the reading had stopped.

Miss Cuyler was very tired. It was close and hot, and her head ached a little, and the prospect across the roofs of the other tenements was not cheerful. Neither was the thought that she was to spend her summer making working-girls happy on a farm on Long Island.

She had grown sceptical as to working-girls, and of the good she did them— or any one else. It was all terribly dreary and forlorn, and she wished she could end it by putting her head on some broad shoulder and by being told that it didn't matter, and that she was not to blame if the world would be wicked and its people unrepentant and ungrateful. Corrigan, on the third floor, was drunk again and promised trouble. His voice ascended to the room in which she sat, and made her nervous, for she was feeling the reaction from the excitement of the night before. There were heavy footsteps on the stairs, and a child's shrill voice cried, "She's in there," and, suspecting it might be Corrigan, she looked up fearfully, and then the door opened and she saw the most magnificent and the handsomest being in the world. His magnificence was due to a Bond Street tailor, who had shown how very small a waist will go with very broad shoulders, and if he was handsome, that was the tan of a week at sea. But it was not the tan, nor the unusual length of his coat, that Eleanore saw, but the eager, confident look in his face—and all she could say was, "Oh, Mr. Wainwright," feebly.

Wainwright waved away all such trifling barriers as "Mister" and "Miss." He came towards her with his face stern and determined. "Eleanore," he said, "I have a hansom at the door, and I want you to come down and get into it."

Was this the young man she had been used to scold and advise and criticise? She looked at him wondering and happy. It seemed to rest her eyes just to see him, and she loved his ordering her so, until a flash of miserable doubt came over her that if he was confident, it was because he was not only sure of himself, but of some one else on the other side of the sea.

And all her pride came to her, and thankfulness that she had not shown him what his coming meant, and she said, "Did my mother send you? How did you come? Is anything wrong?"

He took her hand in one of his and put his other on top of it firmly. "Yes," he said. "Everything is wrong. But we'll fix all that."

He did not seem able to go on immediately, but just looked at her. "Eleanore," he said, "I have been a fool, all sorts of a fool. I came over here to go back again at once, and I am going back, but not alone. I have been alone too long. I had begun to fancy there was only one woman in the world until I came back, and then—something some man said proved to me there was another one, and that she was the only one, and that I—had come near losing her. I had tried to forget about her. I had tried to harden myself to her by thinking she had been hard to me. I said—she does not care for you as the woman you love must care for you, but it doesn't matter now whether she cares or not, for I love *her* so. I want her to come to me and scold me again, and tell me how unworthy I am, and make me good and true like herself, and happy. The rest doesn't count without her, it means nothing to me unless she takes it and keeps it in trust for me, and shares it with me." He had both her hands now, and was pressing them against the flowers in the breast of the long coat.

"Eleanore," he said, "I tried to tell you once of the one thing that would bring me back and you stopped me. Will you stop me now?"

She tried to look up at him, but she would not let him see the happiness in her face just then, and lowered it and gently said, "No, no."

It must have taken him a long time to tell it, for after he had driven them twice around the Park the driver of the hansom decided that he could ask eight dollars at the regular rates, and might even venture on ten, and the result showed that as a judge of human nature he was a success.

They were married in May, and Lord Lowes acted as best man, and his sister sent her warmest congratulations and a pair of silver candlesticks for the dinner-table, which Wainwright thought were very handsome indeed, but which Miss Cuyler considered a little showy. Van Bibber and Travers were ushers, and, indeed, it was Van Bibber himself who closed the door of the carriage upon them as they were starting forth after the wedding. Mrs. Wainwright said something to her husband, and he laughed and said, "Van, Mrs. Wainwright says she's much obliged."

"Yes?" said Van Bibber, pleased and eager, putting his head through the window of the carriage. "What for, Mrs. Wainwright—the chafing-dish? Travers gave half, you know."

And then Mrs. Wainwright said, "No; not for the chafing-dish."

And they drove off, laughing.

"Look at 'em," said Travers, morosely. "*They* don't think the wheels are going around, do they? *They* think it is just the earth revolving with them on top of it, and nobody else. We don't have to say 'please' to no one, not much! We can do just what we jolly well please, and dine when we please and wherever we please. You say to me, Travers, let's go to Pastor's to-night, and I say, I won't, and you say I won't go to the Casino, because I don't want to, and there you are, and all we have to do is to agree to go somewhere else."

"I wonder," said Van Bibber, dreamily, as he watched the carriage disappear down the avenue, "what brings a man to the proposing point?"

"Some other man," said Travers, promptly. "Some man he thinks has more to do for the girl than he likes."

"Who," persisted Van Bibber, innocently, "do you think was the man in that case?"

"How should I know?" exclaimed Travers, impatiently, waving away such unprofitable discussion with a sweep of his stick, and coming down to the serious affairs of life. "What I want to know is to what theatre we are going—that's what I want to know."

A RECRUIT AT CHRISTMAS

Young Lieutenant Claflin left the Brooklyn Navy-yard at an early hour, and arrived at the recruiting-office at ten o'clock. It was the day before Christmas, and even the Bowery, "the thieves' highway," had taken on the emblems and spirit of the season, and the young officer smiled grimly as he saw a hard-faced proprietor of a saloon directing the hanging of wreaths and crosses over the door of his palace and telling the assistant barkeeper to make the red holly berries "show up" better.

The cheap lodging-houses had trailed the green over their illuminated transoms, and even on Mott Street the Chinamen had hung up strings of evergreen over the doors of the joss-house and the gambling-house next door. And the tramps and good-for-nothings, just back from the Island, had an animated, expectant look, as though something certainly was going to happen.

Lieutenant Claflin nodded to Corporal Goddard at the door of the recruiting-office, and startled that veteran's rigidity, and kept his cotton-gloved hand at his visor longer than the Regulations required, by saying, "Wish you merry Christmas," as he jumped up the stairs.

The recruiting-office was a dull, blank-looking place, the view from the windows was not inspiring, and the sight of the plump and black-eyed Jewess in front of the pawn-shop across the street, who was a vision of delight to Corporal Goddard, had no attractions to the officer upstairs. He put on his blue jacket, with the black braid down the front, lighted a cigar, and wrote letters on every other than official matters, and forgot about recruits. He was to have leave of absence on Christmas, and though the others had denounced him for leaving the mess-table on that day, they had forgiven him when he explained that he was going to spend it with his people at home. The others had homes as far away as San Francisco and as far inland as Milwaukee, and some called the big ship of war home; but Claflin's people lived up in Connecticut, and he could reach them in a few hours. He was a very lucky man, the others said, and he felt very cheerful over it, and forgot the blank-looking office with its Rules and Regulations, and colored prints of uniforms, and models of old war-ships, and tin boxes of official documents which were to be filled out and sent to "the Honorable, the Secretary of the Navy."

Corporal Goddard on the stoop below shifted from one foot to the other, and chafed his gloved hands softly together to keep them warm. He had no time to write letters on unofficial writing-paper, nor to smoke cigars or read novels with his feet on a chair, with the choice of looking out at the queer stream of human life moving by below the window on the opposite side of the Bowery. He had to stand straight, which came easily to him now, and to answer questions and urge doubtful minds to join the ranks of the government's marines.

A drunken man gazed at Ogden's colored pictures of the American infantry, cavalry, and marine uniforms that hung before the door, and placed an unsteady finger on the cavalry-man's picture, and said he chose to be one of those. Corporal Goddard told him severely to be off and get sober and grow six inches before he thought of such a thing, and frowned him off the stoop.

Then two boys from the country asked about the service, and went off very quickly when they found they would have to remain in it for three years at least. A great many more stopped in front of the gay pictures and gazed admiringly at Corporal Goddard's bright brass buttons and brilliant complexion, which they innocently attributed to exposure to the sun on long, weary marches. But no one came to offer himself in earnest. At one o'clock Lieutenant Claflin changed his coat and went down-town to luncheon, and came back still more content and in feeling with the season, and lighted another cigar.

But just as he had settled himself comfortably he heard Corporal Goddard's step on the stairs and a less determined step behind him. He took his feet down from the rung of the other chair, pulled his undress jacket into place, and took up a pen.

Corporal Goddard saluted at the door and introduced with a wave of his hand the latest applicant for Uncle Sam's service. The applicant was as young as Lieutenant Claflin, and as good-looking; but he was dirty and unshaven, and his eyes were set back in the sockets, and his fingers twitched at his side. Lieutenant Claflin had seen many applicants in this stage. He called it the remorseful stage, and was used to it.

"Name?" said Lieutenant Claflin, as he pulled a printed sheet of paper towards him.

The applicant hesitated, then he said,

"Walker—John Walker."

The Lieutenant noticed the hesitation, but he merely remarked to himself, "It's none of my business," and added, aloud, "Nationality?" and wrote United States before the applicant answered.

The applicant said he was unmarried, was twenty three years old, and had been born in New York City. Even Corporal Goddard knew this last was not so, but it was none of his business, either. He moved the applicant up against the wall under the measuring-rod, and brought it down on his head.

So he measured and weighed the applicant, and tested his eyesight with printed letters and bits of colored yarn, and the lieutenant kept tally on the sheet, and bit the end of his pen and watched the applicant's face. There were a great many applicants, and few were chosen, but none of them had quite the air about him which this one had. Lieutenant Claflin thought Corporal Goddard was just a bit too callous in the way he handled the applicant, and too peremptory in his questions; but he could not tell why Corporal Goddard treated them all in that way. Then the young officer noticed that the applicant's white face was flushing, and that he bit his lips when Corporal Goddard pushed him towards the weighing-machine as he would have moved a barrel of flour.

"You'll answer," said Lieutenant Claflin, glancing at the sheet. "Your average is very good. All you've got to do now is to sign this, and then it will be over." But he did not let go of the sheet in his hand, as he would have done had he wanted it over. Neither did the applicant move forward to sign.

"After you have signed this," said the young officer, keeping his eyes down on the paper before him, "you will have become a servant of the United States; you will sit in that other room until the office is closed for to-day, and then you will be led over to the Navy-yard and put into a uniform, and from that time on for three years you will have a number, the same number as the one on your musket. You and the musket will both belong to the government. You will clean and load the musket, and fight with it if God ever gives us the chance; and the government will feed you and keep you clean, and fight with you if needful."

The lieutenant looked up at the corporal and said, "You can go, Goddard," and the corporal turned on his heel and walked downstairs, wondering.

"You may spend the three years," continued the officer, still without looking at the applicant, "which are the best years of a young man's life, on the sea, visiting foreign ports, or you may spend it marching up and down the Brooklyn Navy-yard and cleaning brass-work. There are some men who are meant to clean brass-work and to march up and down in front of a stone arsenal, and who are fitted for nothing else. But to every man is given something which should tell him that he is put here to make the best of himself. Every man has that, even the men who are only fit to clean brass rods; but some men kill it, or try to kill it, in different ways, generally by rum. And they are as generally successful, if they keep the process up long enough. The government, of which I am a very humble representative, is always glad to get good men to serve her, but it seems to me (and I may be wrong, and I'm quite sure that I am speaking contrary to Regulations) that some of her men can serve her better in other ways than swabbing down decks. Now, you know yourself best. It may be that you are just the sort of man to stand up and salute the ladies when they come on board to see the ship, and to watch them from for'ard as they walk about with the officers. You won't be allowed to speak to them; you will be number 329 or 328, and whatever benefits a good woman can give a man will be shut off from you, more or less, for three years.

"And, on the other hand, it may be that there are some good women who could keep you on shore, and help you to do something more with yourself than to carry a musket. And, again, it may be that if you stayed on shore you would drink yourself more or less comfortably to death, and break somebody's heart. I can't tell. But if I were not a commissioned officer of the United States, and a thing of Rules and Regulations who can dance and wear a uniform, and a youth generally unfit to pose as an example, I would advise you not to sign this, but to go home and brace up and leave whiskey alone.

"Now, what shall we do?" said the young lieutenant, smiling; "shall we tear this up, or will you sign it?"

The applicant's lips were twitching as well as his hands now, and he rubbed his cuff over his face and smiled back.

"I'm much obliged to you," he said, nervously. "That sounds a rather flat thing to say, I know, but if you knew all I meant by it, though, it would mean enough. I've made a damned fool of myself in this city, but nothing worse. And it was a choice of the navy, where they'd keep me straight, or going to the devil my own way. But it won't be my own way now, thanks to you. I don't know how you saw how it was so quickly; but, you see, I have got a home back in Connecticut, and women that can help me there, and I'll go back to them and ask them to let me start in again where I was when I went away."

"That's good," said the young officer, cheerfully; "that's the way to talk. Tell me where you live in Connecticut, and I'll lend you the car-fare to get there. I'll expect it back with interest, you know," he said, laughing.

"Thank you," said the rejected applicant. "It's not so far but that I can walk, and I don't think you'd believe in me if I took money."

"Oh, yes, I would," said the lieutenant. "How much do you want?"

"Thank you, but I'd rather walk," said the other. "I can get there easily enough by to-morrow. I'll be a nice Christmas present, won't I?" he added, grimly.

"You'll do," said the young officer. "I fancy you'll be about as welcome a one as they'll get." He held out his hand and the other shook it, and walked out with his shoulders as stiff as those of Corporal Goddard.

Then he came back and looked into the room shyly. "I say," he said, hesitatingly. The lieutenant ran his hand down into his pocket. "You've changed your mind?" he asked, eagerly. "That's good. How much will you want?"

The rejected applicant flushed. "No, not that," he said. "I just came back to say—wish you a merry Christmas."

A PATRON OF ART

Young Carstairs and his wife had a studio at Fifty-seventh Street and Sixth Avenue, where Carstairs painted pictures and Mrs. Carstairs mended stockings and wrote letters home to her people in Vermont. Young Carstairs had had a picture in the Salon, and was getting one ready for the Academy, which he hoped to have accepted if he lived long enough to finish it. They were very poor. Not so poor that there was any thought of Carstairs starving to death, but there was at least a possibility that he would not be able to finish his picture in the studio, for which he could not pay the rent. He was very young and had no business to marry; but she was willing, and her people had an idea it would come out all right. They had only three hundred dollars left, and it was mid-winter.

Carstairs went out to sketch Broadway at One Hundred and Fifty-ninth Street, where it is more of a country road than anything else, and his hands almost froze while he was getting down the black lines of the bare trees, and the deep, irregular ruts in the road, where the mud showed through the snow. He intended to put a yellow sky behind this, and a house with smoke coming out of the chimney, and with red light shining through the window, and call it *Winter*.

A horse and buggy stopped just back of him, and he was conscious from the shadows on the snow that the driver was looking down from his perch.

Carstairs paid no attention to his spectator. He was used to working with Park policemen and nursery-maids looking over his shoulder and making audible criticisms or giggling hysterically. So he sketched on and became unconscious of the shadow falling on the snow in front of him; and when he looked up about a quarter of an hour later and noticed that the shadow was still there, he smiled at the tribute such mute attention paid his work. When the sketch was finished he leaned back and closed one eye, and moved his head from side to side and surveyed it critically. Then he heard a voice over his shoulder say, in sympathetic tones, "Purty good, isn't it?" He turned and smiled at his critic, and found him to be a fat, red-faced old gentleman, wrapped in a great fur coat with fur driving-gloves and fur cap.

"You didn't mind my watching you, did you?" asked the old gentleman.

Carstairs said no, he did not mind. The other said that it must be rather cold drawing in such weather, and Carstairs said yes, it was; but that you couldn't get winter and snow in June.

"Exactly," said the driver; "you've got to take it as it comes. How are you going back?"

Carstairs said he would walk to One Hundred and Fifty-fifth Street and take the elevated.

"You'd better get in here," said the older man. "Do you know anything about trotting?" Carstairs got in, and showed that he did know something about trotting by his comments on the mare in front of him. This seemed to please the old gentleman, and he beamed on Carstairs approvingly. He asked him a great many questions about his work, and told him that he owned several good pictures himself, but admitted that it was at his wife's and daughter's suggestion that he had purchased them. "They made me get 'em when we were in Paris," he said, "and they cost a lot of money, and a heap more before I got 'em through the Custom-house." He mentioned the names of the artists who had painted them, and asked Carstairs if he had ever heard of them, and Carstairs said yes, that he knew of them all, and had studied under some of them.

"They're purty high up, I guess," suggested the driver, tentatively.

"Oh, yes," Carstairs answered, lending himself to the other's point of view, "you needn't be afraid of ever losing on your investment. Those pictures will be worth more every year."

This seemed to strike the older man as a very sensible way to take his gallery, and he said, when they had reached the studio, that he would like to see more of Mr. Carstairs and to look at his pictures. His name, he said, was Cole. Carstairs smilingly asked him if he was any relation to the railroad king, of whom the papers spoke as King Cole, and was somewhat embarrassed when the old gentleman replied, gravely, that he was that King Cole himself. Carstairs had a humorous desire to imprison him in his studio and keep him for ransom. Some one held the horse, and the two men went up to the sixth floor and into Carstairs's studio, where they discovered pretty Mrs. Carstairs in the act of sewing a new collar-band on one of her husband's old shirts. She went on at this while the railroad king, who seemed a very simple, kindly old gentleman, wandered around the studio and turned over the pictures, but made no comment. It had been a very cold drive, and Carstairs felt chilled, so he took the hot water his wife had for her tea and some Scotch whiskey and a bit of lemon, and filled a glass with it for his guest and for himself. Mrs. Carstairs rose and put some sugar in King Cole's glass and stirred it for him, and tasted it out of the spoon and coughed, which made the old gentleman laugh. Then he lighted a cigar, and sat back in a big arm-chair and asked many questions, until, before they knew it, the young people had told him a great deal about themselves—almost everything except that they were poor. He could never guess that, they thought, because the studio was so handsomely furnished and in such a proper neighborhood. It was late in the afternoon, and quite dark, when their guest departed, without having made any comment on the paintings he had seen, and certainly without expressing any desire to purchase one.

Mrs. Carstairs said, when her husband told her who their guest had been, that they ought to have held a pistol to his head and made him make out a few checks for them while they had him about. "Billionaires don't drop in like that every day," said she. "I really don't think we appreciated our opportunity."

They were very much surprised a few days later when the railroad king rang at the door, and begged to be allowed to come in and get warm, and to have another glass of hot Scotch. He did this very often, and they got to like him very much. He said he did not care for his club, and his room at home was too strongly suggestive of the shop, on account of the big things he had thought over there, but that their studio was so bright and warm; and they reminded him, he said, of the days when he was first married, before he was rich. They tried to imagine what he was like when he was first married, and failed utterly. Mrs. Carstairs was quite sure he was not at all like her husband.

There was a youth who came to call on the Misses Cole, who had a great deal of money, and who was a dilettante in art. He had had a studio in Paris, where he had spent the last two years, and he wanted one, so he said at dinner one day, in New York.

Old Mr. Cole was seated but one place away from him, and was wondering when the courses would stop and he could get upstairs. He did not care for the dinners his wife gave, but she always made him come to them. He never could remember whether the roast came before or after the bird, and he was trying to guess how much longer it would be before he would be allowed to go, when he overheard the young man at his daughter's side speaking.

"The only studio in the building that I would care to have," said the young man, "is occupied at present. A young fellow named Carstairs has it, but he is going to give it up next week, when I will move in. He has not been successful in getting rid of his pictures, and he and his wife are going back to Vermont to live. I feel rather sorry for the chap, for he is really very clever and only needs a start. It is almost impossible for a young artist to get on here, I imagine, unless he knows people, or unless some one who is known buys his work."

"Yes," said Miss Cole, politely. "Didn't you say you met the Whelen girls before you left Paris? Were they really such a success at Homburg?"

Mr. Cole did not eat any more dinner, but sat thoughtfully until he was allowed to go. Then he went out into the hall, and put on his overcoat and hat.

The Carstairses were dismantling the studio. They had been at it all day, and they were very tired. It seemed so much harder work to take the things down and pack them away than it did to unpack them and put them up in appropriate corners and where they would show to the best advantage.

The studio looked very bare indeed, for the rugs and altar cloths and old curtains had been stripped from the walls, and the pictures and arms and plaques lay scattered all over the floor. It was only a week before Christmas, and it seemed a most inappropriate time to evict one's self. "And it's hardest," said Carstairs, as he rolled up a great Daghestan rug and sat on it, "to go back and own up that you're a failure."

"A what!" cried young Mrs. Carstairs, indignantly. "Aren't you ashamed of yourself? You're not a failure. It's the New Yorkers who don't know what's good when it's shown them. They'll buy all those nasty French pictures because they're expensive and showy, and they can't understand what's true and good. They're not educated up to it, and they won't be for fifty years yet."

"Fifty years is a long time to wait," said her husband, resignedly, "but if necessary we can give them that much time. And we were to have gone abroad, and taken dinner at Bignon's, and had a studio in Montmartre."

"Well, you needn't talk about that just now," said Mrs. Carstairs, as she shook out an old shawl. "It's not cheerful."

There came a knock at the door, and the railroad king walked in, covered with snow. "Goodness me!" exclaimed King Cole, "what are you doing?"

They told him they were going back to Vermont to spend Christmas and the rest of the winter.

"You might have let me know you were going," said the king. "I had something most important to say to you, and you almost gave me the slip."

He seated himself very comfortably and lighted a fat, black cigar, which he chewed as he smoked. "You know," he said, "that I was brought up in Connecticut. I own the old homestead there still, and a tenant of mine lives in it. I've got a place in London, or, I mean, my wife has, and one in Scotland, and one in Brittany, a château, and one in—well, I've a good many here and there. I keep 'em closed till I want 'em. I've never been to the shooting-place in Scotland—my sons go there—nor to the London house, but I have to the French place, and I like it next best to only one other place on earth. Because it's among big trees and on a cliff, where you can see the ships all day, and the girls in colored petticoats catching those little fish you eat with brown bread. I go there in the summer and sit on the cliff, and smoke and feel just as good as though I owned the whole coast and all the sea in sight. I bought a number of pictures of Brittany, and the girls had the place photographed by a fellow from Paris, with the traps in the front yard, and themselves and their friends on the front terrace in groups. But it never seemed to me to be just what I remembered of the place. And so what I want to ask is, if you'll go up to my old place in Connecticut and paint me a picture of it as I used to know it when I was a boy, so that I can have it by me in my room. A picture with the cow-path leading up from the pool at the foot of the hill, and the stone walls, and the corn piled on the fields, and the pumpkins lying around, and the sun setting behind the house. Paint it on one of these cold, snappy afternoons, when your blood tingles and you feel good that you're alive. And when you get through with that, I'd like you to paint me a picture to match it of the château, and as many little sketches of the fishermen, and the girls with the big white hats and bare legs and red petticoats, as you choose. You can live in the homestead till that picture's done, and then you can cross over and live in the château.

"I don't see that there is anything wrong in painting a picture to order, is there? You paint a portrait to order, why shouldn't you paint an old house, or a beautiful castle on a cliff, with the sea beyond it? If you wish, I'll close with you now and call it a bargain."

Mrs. Carstairs had been standing all this time with an unframed picture in one hand, and a dust brush in the other, and her husband had been sitting on the rolled-up Turkish rug and trying not to look at her.

"I'd like to do it very well," he said, simply.

"Well, that's good," replied the railroad king, heartily. "You'll need a retaining fee, I suppose, like lawyers do; and you put your best work on the two pictures and remember what they mean to *me*, and put the spirit of home into them. It's my home you're painting, do you understand? I think you do. That's why I asked you instead of asking any of the others. Now, you know how I feel about it, and you put the feeling into the picture; and as to the price, you ask whatever you please, and you live at my houses and at my expense until the work is done. If I don't see you again," he said, as he laid a check down on the table among the brushes and paint tubes and cigars, "I will wish you a merry Christmas." Then he hurried out and banged the door behind him and escaped their thanks, and left them alone together.

The pictures of Breton life and landscape were exhibited a year later in Paris, and in the winter in New York, and, as they bore the significant numerals of the Salon on the frame, they were immediately appreciated, and many people asked the price. But the attendant said they were already sold to Mr. Cole, the railroad king, who had purchased also the great artistic success of the exhibition—an old farm-house with a wintry landscape, and the word "Home" printed beneath it.

ANDY M'GEE'S CHORUS GIRL

Andy M'Gee was a fireman, and was detailed every evening to theatre duty at the Grand Opera House, where the Ada Howard Burlesque and Comic Opera Company was playing "Pocahontas." He had nothing to do but to stand in the first entrance and watch the border lights and see that the stand lights in the wings did not set fire to the canvas. He was a quiet, shy young man, very strong-looking and with a handsome boyish face. Miss Agnes Carroll was the third girl from the right in the first semi-circle of amazons, and very beautiful. By rights she should have been on the end, but she was so proud and haughty that she would smile but seldom, and never at the men in front. Brady, the stage manager, who was also the second comedian, said that a girl on the end should at least look as though she were enjoying herself, and though he did not expect her to talk across the footlights, she might at least look over them once in a while, just to show there was no ill feeling. Miss Carroll did not agree with him in this, and so she was relegated to the third place, and another girl who was more interested in the audience and less in the play took her position. When Miss Carroll was not on the stage she used to sit on the carpeted steps of the throne, which were not in use after the opening scene, and read novels by the Duchess, or knit on a pair of blue woollen wristlets, which she kept wrapped up in a towel and gave to the wardrobe woman to hold when she went on. One night there was a quicker call than usual, owing to Ada Howard's failing to get her usual encore for her waltz song, and Brady hurried them. The wardrobe woman was not in sight, so Agnes handed her novel and her knitting to M'Gee and said: "Will you hold these for me until I come off?" She looked at him for the first time as she handed him the things, and he felt, as he had felt several times before, that her beauty was of a distinctly disturbing quality. There was something so shy about her face when she was not on the stage, and something so kindly, that he stood holding the pieces of blue wool, still warm from her hands, without moving from the position he had held when she gave them to him. When she came off he gave them back to her and touched the visor of his cap as she thanked him. One of the other beautiful amazons laughed and whispered, "Agnes has a mash on the fire laddie," which made the retiring Mr. M'Gee turn very red. He did not dare to look and see what effect it had on Miss Carroll. But the next evening he took off his hat to her, and she said "Good-evening," quite boldly. After that he watched her a great deal. He thought he did it in such a way that she did not see him, but that was only because he was a man; for the other women noticed it at once, and made humorous comments on it when they were in the dressing-rooms.

Old man Sanders, who had been in the chorus of different comic-opera companies since he was twenty years old, and who was something of a pessimist, used to take great pleasure in abusing the other members of the company to Andy M'Gee, and in telling anecdotes concerning them which were extremely detrimental to their characters. He could not find anything good to say of any of them, and M'Gee began to believe that the stage was a very terrible place indeed. He was more sorry for this, and he could not at first understand why, until he discovered that he was very much interested in Miss Agnes Carroll, and her character was to him a thing of great and poignant importance. He often wished to ask old Sanders about her, but he was afraid to do so, partly because he thought he ought to take it for granted that she was a good girl, and partly because he was afraid Sanders would tell him she was not. But one night as she passed them, as proud and haughty looking as ever, old Sanders grunted scornfully, and M'Gee felt that he was growing very red.

"Now, there is a girl," said the old man, "who ought to be out of this business. She's too good for it, and she'll never get on in it. Not that she couldn't keep straight and get on, but because she is too little interested in it, and shows no heart in the little she has to do. She can sing a little bit, but she can't do the steps."

"Then why does she stay in it?" said Andy M'Gee.

"Well, they tell me she's got a brother to support. He's too young or too lazy to work, or a cripple or something. She tried giving singing lessons, but she couldn't get any pupils, and now she supports herself and her brother with this."

Andy M'Gee felt a great load lifted off his mind. He became more and more interested in Miss Agnes Carroll, and he began to think up little speeches to make to her, which were intended to show how great his respect for her was, and what an agreeable young person he might be if you only grew to know him. But she never grew to know him. She always answered him very quietly and very kindly, but never with any show of friendliness or with any approach to it, and he felt that he would never know her any better than he did on the first night she spoke to him. But three or four times he found her watching him, and he took heart at this and from something he believed he saw in her manner and in the very reticence she showed. He counted up how much of his pay he had saved, and concluded that with it and with what he received monthly he could very well afford to marry. When he decided on this he became more devoted to her, and even the girls stopped laughing about it now. They saw it was growing very serious indeed.

One afternoon there was a great fire, and he and three others fell from the roof and were burned a bit, and the boy ambulance surgeon lost his head and said they were seriously injured, which fact got into the afternoon papers, and when Andy turned up as usual at the Opera House there was great surprise and much rejoicing. And the next day one of the wounded firemen who had had to remain in the hospital overnight told Andy that a most beautiful lady had come there and asked to see him and had then said: "This is not the man; the papers said Mr. M'Gee was hurt." She had refused to tell her name, but had gone away greatly relieved.

Andy dared to think that this had been Agnes Carroll, and that night he tried to see her to speak to her, but she avoided him and went at once to her dressing-room whenever she was off the stage. But Andy was determined to speak to her, and waited for her at the stage door, instead of going back at once to the engine house to make out his report, which was entirely wrong, and which cost him a day's pay. It was Tuesday night, and salaries had just been given all around, and the men and girls left the stage door with the envelopes in their hands and discussing the different restaurants at which they would fitly celebrate the weekly walk of the ghost. Agnes came out among the last, veiled, and moving quickly through the crowd of half-grown boys, and men about town, and poor relations who lay in wait and hovered around the lamp over the stage door like moths about a candle. Andy stepped forward quickly to follow her, but before he could reach her side a man stepped up to her, and she stopped and spoke to him in a low tone and retreated as she spoke. Andy heard him, with a sharp, jealous doubt in his heart, and stood still. Then the man reached for the envelope in the girl's hand and said, "Give it to me, do you hear?" and she drew back and started to run, but he seized her arm. Then Andy jumped at him and knocked him down, and picked him up again by the collar and beat him over the head. "Stop!" the girl cried. "Stop!"

"Stop like—," said Andy.

"Stop! do you hear?" cried the woman again "He has a right to the money. He is my husband."

Andy asked to be taken off theatre duty, and the captain did what he asked. After that he grew very morose and unhappy, and was as cross and disagreeable as he could be; so that the other men said they would like to thrash him just once. But when there was a fire he acted like another man, and was so reckless that the captain, mistaking foolhardiness for bravery, handed in his name for promotion, and as his political backing was very strong, he was given the white helmet and became foreman of another engine-house. But he did not seem to enjoy life any the more, and he was most unpopular. The winter passed away and the summer came, and one day on Fifth Avenue Andy met old man Sanders, whom he tried to avoid, because the recollections he brought up were bitter ones; but Sanders buttonholed him and told him he had been reading about his getting the Bennett medal, and insisted on his taking a drink with him.

"And, by the way," said Sanders, just as Andy thought he had finally succeeded in shaking him off, "do you remember Agnes Carroll? It seems she was married to a drunken, good-for-nothing lout, who beat her. Well, he took a glass too much one night, and walked off a ferry-boat into the East River. Drink is a terrible thing, isn't it? They say the paddle-wheels knocked the—"

"And his wife?" gasped Andy.

"She's with us yet," said Sanders. "We're at the Bijou this week. Come in and see the piece."

Brady, the stage manager, waved a letter at the acting manager.

"Letter from Carroll," he said. "Sends in her notice. Going to leave the stage, she says; going to get married again. She was a good girl," he added with a sigh, "and she sang well enough, but she couldn't do the dance steps a little bit."

A LEANDER OF THE EAST RIVER

"Hefty" Burke was one of the best swimmers in the East River. There was no regular way open for him to prove this, as the gentlemen of the Harlem boat-clubs, under whose auspices the annual races were given, called him a professional, and would not swim against him. "They won't keep company with me on land," Hefty complained, bitterly, "and they can't keep company with me in the water; so I lose both ways." Young Burke held these gentlemen of the rowing clubs in great contempt, and their outriggers and low-necked and picturesque rowing clothes as well. They were fond of lying out of the current, with the oars pulled across at their backs for support, smoking and commenting audibly upon the other oarsmen who passed them by perspiring uncomfortably, and conscious that they were being criticised. Hefty said that these amateur oarsmen and swimmers were only pretty boys, and that he could give them two hundred yards start in a mile of rough or smooth water and pass them as easily as a tug passes a lighter.

He was quite right in this latter boast; but, as they would call him a professional and would not swim against him, there was no way for him to prove it. His idea of a race and their idea of a race differed. They had a committee to select prizes and open a book for entries, and when the day of the races came they had a judges' boat with gay bunting all over it, and a badly frightened referee and a host of reporters, and police boats to keep order. But when Hefty swam, his two backers, who had challenged some other young man through a sporting paper, rowed in a boat behind him and yelled and swore directions, advice, warnings, and encouragement at him, and in their excitement drank all of the whiskey that had been intended for him. And the other young man's backers, who had put up ten dollars on him, and a tugboat filled with other rough young men, kegs of beer, and three Italians with two fiddles and one harp, followed close in the wake of the swimmers. It was most exciting, and though Hefty never had any prizes to show for it, he always came in first, and so won a great deal of local reputation. He also gained renown as a life-saver; for if it had not been for him many a venturesome lad would have ended his young life in the waters of the East River.

For this he received ornate and very thin gold medals, with very little gold spread over a large extent of medal, from grateful parents and admiring friends. These were real medals, and given to him, and not paid for by himself as were "Rags" Raegan's, who always bought himself a medal whenever he assaulted a reputable citizen and the case was up before the Court of General Sessions. It was the habit of Mr. Raegan's friends to fall overboard for him whenever he was in difficulty of this sort, and allow themselves to be saved, and to present Raegan with the medal he had prepared; and this act of heroism would get into the papers, and Raegan's lawyer would make the most of it before the judges. Rags had been Hefty's foremost rival among the swimmers of the East Side, but since the retirement of the former into reputable and private life Hefty was the acknowledged champion of the river front.

Hefty was not at all a bad young man—that is, he did not expect his people to support him—and he worked occasionally, especially about election time, and what he made in bets and in backing himself to swim supplied him with small change. Then he fell in love with Miss Casey, and the trouble and happiness of his life came to him hand and hand together; and as this human feeling does away with class distinctions, I need not feel I must apologize for him any longer, but just tell his story.

He met her at the Hon. P.C. McGovern's Fourth Ward Association's excursion and picnic, at which he was one of the twenty-five vice-presidents. On this occasion Hefty had jumped overboard after one of the Rag Gang whom the members of the Half-Hose Social Club had, in a spirit of merriment, dropped over the side of the boat. This action and the subsequent rescue and ensuing intoxication of the half-drowned member of the Rag Gang had filled Miss Casey's heart with admiration, and she told Hefty he was a good one and ought to be proud of himself.

On the following Sunday he walked out Avenue A to Tompkins Square with Mary, and he also spent a great deal of time every day on her stoop when he was not working, for he was working now and making ten dollars a week as an assistant to an ice-driver. They had promised to give him fifteen dollars a week and a seat on the box if he proved steady. He had even dreamed of wedding Mary in the spring. But Casey was a particularly objectionable man for a father-in-law, and his objections to Hefty were equally strong. He honestly thought the young man no fit match for his daughter, and would only promise to allow him to "keep company" with Mary on the condition of his living steadily.

So it became Hefty's duty to behave himself. He found this a little hard to do at first, but he confessed that it grew easier as he saw more of Miss Casey. He attributed his reform to her entirely. She had made the semi-political, semi-social organizations to which he belonged appear stupid, and especially so when he lost his money playing poker in the club-room (for the club had only one room), when he might have put it away for her. He liked to talk with her about the neighbors in the tenement, and his chance of political advancement to the position of a watchman at the Custom-house Wharf, and hear her play "Mary and John" on the melodeon. He boasted that she could make it sound as well as it did on the barrel-organ.

He was very polite to her father and very much afraid of him, for he was a most particular old man from the North of Ireland, and objected to Hefty because he was a good Catholic and fond of street fights. He also asked pertinently how Hefty expected to support a wife by swimming from one pier to another on the chance of winning ten dollars, and pointed out that even this precarious means of livelihood would be shut off when the winter came. He much preferred "Patsy" Moffat as a prospective son-in-law, because Moffat was one of the proprietors in a local express company with a capital stock of three wagons and two horses. Miss Casey herself, so it seemed to Hefty, was rather fond of Moffat; but he could not tell for whom she really cared, for she was very shy, and would as soon have thought of speaking a word of encouragement as of speaking with unkindness.

There was to be a ball at the Palace Garden on Wednesday night, and Hefty had promised to call for Mary at nine o'clock. She told him to be on time, and threatened to go with her old love, Patsy Moffat, if he were late.

On Monday night the foreman at the livery stable of the ice company appointed Hefty a driver, and, as his wages would now be fifteen dollars a week, he concluded to ask Mary to marry him on Wednesday night at the dance.

He was very much elated and very happy.

His fellow-workmen heard of his promotion and insisted on his standing treat, which he did several times, until the others became flippant in their remarks and careless in their conduct. In this innocent but somewhat noisy state they started home, and on the way were injudicious enough to say, "Ah there!" to a policeman as he issued from the side door of a saloon. The policeman naturally pounded the nearest of them on the head with his club, and as Hefty happened to be that one, and as he objected, he was arrested. He gave a false name, and next morning pleaded not guilty to the charge of "assaulting an officer and causing a crowd to collect."

His sentence was thirty days in default of three hundred dollars, and by two o'clock he was on the boat to the Island, and by three he had discarded the blue shirt and red suspenders of an iceman for the gray stiff cloth of a prisoner. He took the whole trouble terribly to heart. He knew that if Old Man Casey, as he called him, heard of it there would be no winning his daughter with his consent, and he feared that the girl herself would have grave doubts concerning him. He was especially cast down when he thought of the dance on Wednesday night, and of how she would go off with Patsy Moffat. And what made it worse was the thought that if he did not return he would lose his position at the ice company's stable, and then marriage with Mary would be quite impossible. He grieved over this all day, and speculated as to what his family would think of him. His circle of friends was so well known to other mutual friends that he did not dare to ask any of them to bail him out, for this would have certainly come to Casey's ears.

He could do nothing but wait. And yet thirty days was a significant number to his friends, and an absence of that duration would be hard to explain. On Wednesday morning, two days after his arrest, he was put to work with a gang of twenty men breaking stone on the roadway that leads from the insane quarters to the penitentiary. It was a warm, sunny day, and the city, lying just across the narrow channel, never looked more beautiful. It seemed near enough for him to reach out his hand and touch it. And the private yachts and big excursion-boats that passed, banging out popular airs and alive with bunting, made Hefty feel very bitter. He determined that when he got back he would go look up the policeman who had assaulted him and break his head with a brick in a stocking. This plan cheered him somewhat, until he thought again of Mary Casey at the dance that night with Patsy Moffat, and this excited him so that he determined madly to break away and escape. His first impulse was to drop his crowbar and jump into the river on the instant, but his cooler judgment decided him to wait.

At the northern end of the Island the grass runs high, and there are no houses of any sort upon it. It reaches out into a rocky point, where it touches the still terribly swift eddies of Hell Gate, and its sharp front divides the water and directs it towards Astoria on the east and the city on the west. Hefty determined to walk off from the gang of workmen until he could drop into this grass and to lie there until night. This would be easy, as there was only one man to watch them, for they were all there for only ten days or one month, and the idea that they should try to escape was hardly considered. So Hefty edged off farther from the gang, and then, while the guard was busy lighting his pipe, dropped into the long grass and lay there quietly, after first ridding himself of his shoes and jacket. At six o'clock a bell tolled and the guard marched away, with his gang shambling after him. Hefty guessed they would not miss him until they came to count heads at supper-time; but even now it was already dark, and lights were showing on the opposite bank. He had selected the place he meant to swim for—a green bank below a row of new tenements, a place where a few bushes still stood, and where the boys of Harlem hid their clothes when they went in swimming.

At half-past seven it was quite dark, so dark, in fact, that the three lanterns which came tossing towards him told Hefty that his absence had been discovered. He rose quickly and stepped cautiously, instead of diving, into the river, for he was fearful of hidden rocks. The current was much stronger than he had imagined, and he hesitated for a moment, with the water pulling at his knees, but only for a moment; for the men were hunting for him in the grass.

He drew the gray cotton shirt from his shoulders, and threw it back of him with an exclamation of disgust, and of relief at being a free man again, and struck his broad, bare chest and the biceps of his arms with a little gasp of pleasure in their perfect strength, and then bent forward and slid into the river.

The current from the opening at Hell Gate caught him up as though he had been a plank. It tossed him and twisted him and sucked him down. He beat his way for a second to the surface and gasped for breath and was drawn down again, striking savagely at the eddies which seemed to twist his limbs into useless, heavy masses of flesh and muscle. Then he dived down and down, seeking a possibly less rapid current at the muddy bottom of the river; but the current drew him up again until he reached the top, just in time, so it seemed to him, to breathe the pure air before his lungs split with the awful pressure. He was gloriously and fiercely excited by the unexpected strength of his opponent and the probably fatal outcome of his adventure. He stopped struggling, that he might gain fresh strength, and let the current bear him where it would, until he saw that it was carrying him swiftly to the shore and to the rocks of the Island. And then he dived again and beat his way along the bottom, clutching with his hands at the soft, thick mud, and rising only to gasp for breath and sink again. His eyes were smarting hotly, and his head and breast ached with pressure that seemed to come from the inside and threatened to burst its way out. His arms had grown like lead and had lost their strength, and his legs were swept and twisted away from his control and were numb and useless. He assured himself fiercely that he could not have been in the water for more than five minutes at the longest, and reminded himself that he had often before lived in it for hours, and that this power, which was so much greater than his own, could not outlast him. But there was no sign of abatement in the swift, cruel uncertainty of its movement, and it bore him on and down or up as it pleased. The lights on the shore became indistinct, and he finally confused the two shores, and gave up hope of reaching the New York side, except by accident, and hoped only to reach some solid land alive. He did not go over all of his past life, but the vision of Mary Casey did come to him, and how she would not know that he had been innocent. It was a little thing to distress himself about at such a time, but it hurt him keenly. And then the lights grew blurred, and he felt that he was making heavy mechanical strokes that barely kept his lips above the water-line. He felt the current slacken perceptibly, but he was too much exhausted to take advantage of it, and drifted forward with it, splashing feebly like a dog, and holding his head back with a desperate effort. A huge, black shadow, only a shade blacker than the water around him, loomed up suddenly on his right, and he saw a man's face appear in the light of a hatchway and disappear again.

"Help!" he cried, "help!" but his voice sounded far away and barely audible. He struck out desperately against the current, and turned on his back and tried to keep himself afloat where he was. "Help!" he called again, feebly, grudging the strength it took to call even that. "Help! Quick, for God's sake! help me!"

Something heavy, black, and wet struck him sharply in the face and fell with a splash on the water beside him. He clutched for it quickly, and clasped it with both hands and felt it grow taut; and then gave up thinking, and they pulled him on board.

When he came to himself, the captain of the canal-boat stooped and took a fold of the gray trousers between his thumb and finger. Then he raised his head and glanced across at the big black Island, where lights were still moving about on the shore, and whistled softly. But Hefty looked at him so beseechingly that he arose and came back with a pair of old boots and a suit of blue jeans.

"Will you send these back to me to-morrow?" he asked.

"Sure," said Hefty.

"And what'll I do with these?" said the captain, holding up the gray trousers.

"Anything you want, except to wear 'em," said Mr. Burke, feebly, with a grin.

One hour later Miss Casey was standing up with Mr. Patsy Moffat for the grand march of the grand ball of the Jolly Fellows' Pleasure Club of the Fourteenth Ward, held at the Palace Garden. The band was just starting the "Boulanger March," and Mr. Moffat was saying wittily that it was warm enough to eat ice, when Mr. Hefty Burke shouldered in between him and Miss Casey. He was dressed in his best suit of clothes, and his hair was conspicuously damp.

"Excuse me, Patsy," said Mr. Burke, as he took Miss Casey's arm, in his, "but this march is promised to me. I'm sorry I was late, and I'm sorry to disappoint you; but you're like the lad that drives the hansom cab, see?—you're not in it."

"But indeed," said Miss Casey, later, "you shouldn't have kept me a-waiting. It wasn't civil."

"I know," assented Hefty, gloomily, "but I came as soon as I could. I even went widout me supper so's to get here; an' they wuz expectin' me to stay to supper, too."

HOW HEFTY BURKE GOT EVEN

Hefty Burke was once clubbed by a policeman named McCluire, who excused the clubbing to his Honor by swearing that Hefty had been drunk and disorderly, which was not true. Hefty got away from the Island by swimming the East River, and swore to get even with the policeman. This story tells how he got even.

Mr. Carstairs was an artist who had made his first great success by painting figures and landscapes in Brittany. He had a studio at Fifty-eighth Street and Sixth Avenue, and was engaged on an historical subject in which there were three figures. One was a knight in full armor, and the other was a Moor, and the third was the figure of a woman. The suit of armor had been purchased by Mr. Carstairs in Paris, and was believed to have been worn by a brave nobleman, one of whose extravagant descendants had sold everything belonging to his family in order to get money with which to play baccarat. Carstairs was at the sale and paid a large price for the suit of armor which the Marquis de Neuville had worn, and set it up in a corner of his studio. It was in eight or a dozen pieces, and quite heavy, but was wonderfully carved and inlaid with silver, and there were dents on it that showed where a Saracen's scimetar had been dulled and many a brave knight's spear had struck. Mr. Carstairs had paid so much for it that he thought he ought to make a better use of it, if possible, than simply to keep it dusted and show it off to his friends. So he began this historical picture, and engaged Hefty Burke to pose as the knight and wear the armor. Hefty's features were not exactly the sort of features you would imagine a Marquis de Neuville would have; but as his visor was down in the picture, it did not make much material difference; and as his figure was superb, he answered very well. Hefty drove an ice-wagon during business hours, and, as a personal favor to Mr. Carstairs, agreed to pose for him, for a consideration, two afternoons of each week, and to sleep in the studio at night, for it was filled with valuable things.

The armor was a never-ending source of amazement and bewilderment to Hefty. He could not understand why a man would wear such a suit, and especially when he went out to fight. It was the last thing in the world he would individually have selected in which to make war.

"Ef I was goin' to scrap wid anybody," he said to Mr. Carstairs, "I'd as lief tie meself up wid dumb-bells as take to carry all this stuff on me. A man wid a baseball bat and swimmin' tights on could dance all around youse and knock spots out of one of these things. The other lad wouldn't be in it. Why, before he could lift his legs or get his hands up you cud hit him on his helmet, and he wouldn't know what killed him. They must hev sat down to fight in them days."

Mr. Carstairs painted on in silence and smiled grimly.

"I'd like to have seen a go with the parties fixed out in a pair of these things," continued Hefty. "I'd bet on the lad that got in the first whack. He wouldn't have to do nothing but shove the other one over on his back and fall on him. Why, I guess this weighs half a ton if it weighs an ounce!"

For all his contempt, Hefty had a secret admiration for the ancient marquis who had worn this suit, and had been strong enough to carry its weight and demolish his enemies besides. The marks on the armor interested him greatly, and he was very much impressed one day when he found what he declared to be blood-stains on the lining of the helmet.

"I guess the old feller that wore this was a sport, eh?" he said, proudly, shaking the pieces on his arms until they rattled. "I guess he done 'em up pretty well for all these handicaps. I'll bet when he got to falling around on 'em and butting 'em with this fire helmet he made 'em purty tired. Don't youse think so?"

Young Carstairs said he didn't doubt it for a moment.

The Small Hours Social Club was to give a prize masquerade ball at the Palace Garden on New Year's Night, and Hefty had decided to go. Every gentleman dancer was to get a white silk badge with a gold tassel, and every committeeman received a blue badge with "Committee" written across it in brass letters. It cost three dollars to be a committeeman, but only one dollar "for self and lady." There were three prizes. One of a silver water-pitcher for the "handsomest-costumed lady dancer," an accordion for the "best-dressed gent," and a cake for the most original idea in costume, whether worn by "gent or lady." Hefty, as well as many others, made up his mind to get the accordion, if it cost him as much as seven dollars, which was half of his week's wages. It wasn't the prize he wanted so much, but he thought of the impression it would make on Miss Casey, whose father was the well-known janitor of that name. They had been engaged for some time, but the engagement hung fire, and Hefty thought that a becoming and appropriate costume might hasten matters a little. He was undecided as to whether he should go as an Indian or as a courtier of the time of Charles II. Auchmuty Stein, of the Bowery, who supplies costumes and wigs at reasonable rates, was of the opinion that a neat sailor suit of light blue silk and decorated with white anchors was about the "brettiest thing in the shop, and sheap at fife dollars;" but Hefty said he never saw a sailor in silk yet, and he didn't think they ever wore it. He couldn't see how they could keep the tar and salt-water from ruining it.

The Charles II. court suit was very handsome, and consisted of red cotton tights, blue velveteen doublet, and a blue cloak lined with pale pink silk. A yellow wig went with this, and a jewelled sword which would not come out of the scabbard. It could be had for seven dollars a night. Hefty was still in doubt about it and was much perplexed. Auchmuty Stein told him Charlie Macklin, the Third Avenue ticket-chopper, was after the same suit, and that he had better take it while he could get it. But Hefty said he'd think about it. The next day was his day for posing, and as he stood arrayed in the Marquis de Neuville's suit of mail he chanced to see himself in one of the long mirrors, and was for the first time so struck with the ferocity of his appearance that he determined to see if old man Stein had not a suit of imitation armor, which would not be so heavy and would look as well. But the more Hefty thought of it, the more he believed that only the real suit would do. Its associations, its blood-stains, and the real silver tracings haunted him, and he half decided to ask Mr. Carstairs to lend it to him.

But then he remembered overhearing Carstairs tell a brother-artist that he had paid two thousand francs for it, and, though he did not know how much a franc might be, two thousand of anything was too much to wear around at a masquerade ball. But the thing haunted him. He was sure if Miss Casey saw him in that suit she would never look at Charlie Macklin again.

"They wouldn't be in the same town with me," said Hefty. "And I'd get two of the prizes, sure."

He was in great perplexity, when good luck or bad luck settled it for him.

"Burke," said Mr. Carstairs, "Mrs. Carstairs and I are going out of town for New Year's Day, and will be gone until Sunday. Take a turn through the rooms each night, will you? as well as the studio, and see that everything is all right." That clinched the matter for Hefty. He determined to go as far as the Palace Garden as the Marquis de Neuville, and say nothing whatever to Mr. Carstairs about it.

Stuff McGovern, who drove a night-hawk and who was a particular admirer of Hefty's, even though as a cabman he was in a higher social scale than the driver of an ice-cart, agreed to carry Hefty and his half-ton of armor to the Garden, and call for him when the ball was over.

"Holee smoke!" gasped Mr. McGovern, as Hefty stumbled heavily across the pavement with an overcoat over his armor and his helmet under his arm. "Do you expect to do much dancing in that sheet-iron?"

"It's the looks of the thing I'm gambling on," said Hefty. "I look like a locomoteeve when I get this stovepipe on me head."

Hefty put on his helmet in the cab and pulled down the visor, and when he alighted the crowd around the door was too greatly awed to jeer, but stood silent with breathless admiration. He had great difficulty in mounting the somewhat steep flight of stairs which led to the dancing-room, and considered gloomily that in the event of a fire he would have a very small chance of getting out alive. He made so much noise coming up that the committeemen thought some one was rolling some one else down the stairs, and came out to see the fight. They observed Hefty's approach with whispered awe and amazement.

"Wot are you?" asked the man at the door. "Youse needn't give your real name," he explained, politely. "But you've got to give something if youse are trying for a prize, see?"

"I'm the Black Knight," said Hefty in a hoarse voice, "the Marquis de Newveal; and when it comes to scrappin' wid der perlice, I'm de best in der business."

This last statement was entirely impromptu, and inspired by the presence of Policeman McCluire, who, with several others, had been detailed to keep order. McCluire took this challenge calmly, and looked down and smiled at Hefty's feet.

"He looks like a stove on two legs," he said to the crowd. The crowd, as a matter of policy, laughed.

"You'll look like a fool standing on his head in a snow-bank if you talk impudent to me," said Hefty, epigrammatically, from behind the barrier of his iron mask. What might have happened next did not happen, because at that moment the music sounded for the grand march, and Hefty and the policeman were swept apart by the crowd of Indians, Mexicans, courtiers, negro minstrels, and clowns. Hefty stamped across the waxed floor about as lightly as a safe could do it if a safe could walk. He found Miss Casey after the march and disclosed his identity. She promised not to tell, and was plainly delighted and flattered at being seen with the distinct sensation of the ball. "Say, Hefty," she said, "they just ain't in it with you. You'll take the two prizes sure. How do I look?"

"Out o' sight," said Hefty. "Never saw you lookin' better."

"That's good," said Miss Casey, simply, and with a sigh of satisfaction.

Hefty was undoubtedly a great success. The men came around him and pawed him, and felt the dents in the armor, and tried the weight of it by holding up one of his arms, and handled him generally as though he were a freak in a museum. "Let 'em alone," said Hefty to Miss Casey, "I'm not sayin' a word. Let the judges get on to the sensation I'm a-makin,' and I'll walk off with the prizes. The crowd is wid me sure."

At midnight the judges pounded on a table for order, and announced that after much debate they gave the first prize to Miss Lizzie Cannon, of Hester Street, for "having the most handsomest costume on the floor, that of Columbia." The fact that Mr. "Buck" Masters, who was one of the judges, and who was engaged to Miss Cannon, had said that he would pound things out of the other judges if they gave the prize elsewhere was not known, but the decision met with as general satisfaction as could well be expected.

"The second prize," said the judges, "goes to the gent calling himself the Black Knight—him in the iron leggings—and the other prize for the most original costume goes to him, too." Half the crowd cheered at this, and only one man hissed. Hefty, filled with joy and with the anticipation of the elegance the ice-pitcher would lend to his flat when he married Miss Casey, and how conveniently he could fill it, turned on this gentleman and told him that only geese hissed.

The gentleman, who had spent much time on his costume, and who had been assured by each judge on each occasion that evening when he had treated him to beer that he would get the prize, told Hefty to go lie down. It has never been explained just what horrible insult lies back of this advice, but it is a very dangerous thing to tell a gentleman to do. Hefty lifted one foot heavily and bore down on the disappointed masker like an ironclad in a heavy sea. But before he could reach him Policeman McCluire, mindful of the insult put upon him by this stranger, sprang between them and said: "Here, now, no scrapping here; get out of this," and shoved Hefty back with his hand. Hefty uttered a mighty howl of wrath and long-cherished anger, and lurched forward, but before he could reach his old-time enemy three policemen had him around the arms and by the leg, and he was as effectually stopped as though he had been chained to the floor.

"Let go o' me," said Hefty, wildly. "You're smotherin' me. Give me a fair chance at him."

But they would not give him any sort of a chance. They rushed him down the steep stairs, and while McCluire ran ahead two more pushed back the crowd that had surged uncertainly forward to the rescue. If Hefty had declared his identity the police would have had a very sad time of it; but that he must not get Mr. Carstairs's two-thousand-franc suit into trouble was all that filled Hefty's mind, and all that he wanted was to escape. Three policemen walked with him down the street. They said they knew where he lived, and that they were only going to take him home. They said this because they were afraid the crowd would interfere if it imagined Hefty was being led to the precinct station-house.

But Hefty knew where he was going as soon as he turned the next corner and was started off in the direction of the station-house. There was still quite a small crowd at his heels, and Stuff McGovern was driving along at the side anxious to help, but fearful to do anything, as Hefty had told him not to let any one know who his fare had been and that his incognito must be preserved.

The blood rushed to Hefty's head like hot liquor. To be arrested for nothing, and by that thing McCluire, and to have the noble coat-of-mail of the Marquis de Neuville locked up in a dirty cell and probably ruined, and to lose his position with Carstairs, who had always treated him so well, it was terrible! It could not be! He looked through his visor; to the right and to the left a policeman walked on each side of him with his hand on his iron sleeve, and McCluire marched proudly before. The dim lamps of McGovern's night-hawk shone at the side of the procession and showed the crowd trailing on behind. Suddenly Hefty threw up his visor "Stuff," he cried, "are youse with me?"

He did not wait for any answer, but swung back his two iron arms and then brought them forward with a sweep on to the back of the necks of the two policemen. They went down and forward as if a lamp-post had fallen on them, but were up again in a second. But before they could rise Hefty set his teeth, and with a gurgle of joy butted his iron helmet into McCluire's back and sent him flying forward into a snow-bank. Then he threw himself on him and buried him under three hundred pounds of iron and flesh and blood, and beat him with his mailed hand over the head and choked the snow and ice down into his throat and nostrils.

"You'll club me again, will you?" he cried. "You'll send me to the Island?" The two policemen were pounding him with their night-sticks as effectually as though they were rapping on a door-step; and the crowd, seeing this, fell on them from behind, led by Stuff McGovern with his whip, and rolled them in the snow and tried to tear off their coat-tails, which means money out of the policeman's own pocket for repairs, and hurts more than broken ribs, as the Police Benefit Society pays for them.

"Now then, boys, get me into a cab," cried Hefty. They lifted him in and obligingly blew out the lights so that the police could not see its number, and Stuff drove Hefty proudly home. "I guess I'm even with that cop now," said Hefty as he stood at the door of the studio building perspiring and happy; "but if them cops ever find out who the Black Knight was, I'll go away for six months on the Island. I guess," he added, thoughtfully, "I'll have to give them two prizes up."

OUTSIDE THE PRISON

It was about ten o'clock on the night before Christmas, and very cold. Christmas Eve is a very-much-occupied evening everywhere, in a newspaper office especially so, and all of the twenty and odd reporters were out that night on assignments, and Conway and Bronson were the only two remaining in the local room. They were the very best of friends, in the office and out of it; but as the city editor had given Conway the Christmas-eve story to write instead of Bronson, the latter was jealous, and their relations were strained. I use the word "story" in the newspaper sense, where everything written for the paper is a story, whether it is an obituary, or a reading notice, or a dramatic criticism, or a descriptive account of the crowded streets and the lighted shop-windows of a Christmas Eve. Conway had finished his story quite half an hour before, and should have sent it out to be mutilated by the blue pencil of a copy editor; but as the city editor had twice appeared at the door of the local room, as though looking for some one to send out on another assignment, both Conway and Bronson kept on steadily writing against time, to keep him off until some one else came in. Conway had written his concluding paragraph a dozen times, and Bronson had conscientiously polished and repolished a three-line "personal" he was writing, concerning a gentleman unknown to fame, and who would remain unknown to fame until that paragraph appeared in print.

The city editor blocked the door for the third time, and looked at Bronson with a faint smile of sceptical appreciation.

"Is that very important?" he asked.

Bronson said, "Not very," doubtfully, as though he did not think his opinion should be trusted on such a matter, and eyed the paragraph with critical interest. Conway rushed his pencil over his paper, with the tip of his tongue showing between his teeth, and became suddenly absorbed.

"Well, then, if you are not *very* busy," said the city editor, "I wish you would go down to Moyamensing. They release that bank-robber Quinn to-night, and it ought to make a good story. He was sentenced for six years, I think, but he has been commuted for good conduct and bad health. There was a preliminary story about it in the paper this morning, and you can get all the facts from that. It's Christmas Eve, and all that sort of thing, and you ought to be able to make something of it."

There are certain stories written for a Philadelphia newspaper that circle into print with the regularity of the seasons. There is the "First Sunday in the Park," for example, which comes on the first warm Sunday in the spring, and which is made up of a talk with a park policeman who guesses at the number of people who have passed through the gates that day, and announcements of the re-painting of the boat-houses and the near approach of the open-air concerts. You end this story with an allusion to the presence in the park of the "wan-faced children of the tenement," and the worthy workingmen (if it is a one-cent paper which the workingmen are likely to read), and tell how they worshipped nature in the open air, instead of saying that in place of going properly to church, they sat around in their shirt-sleeves and scattered egg-shells and empty beer bottles and greasy Sunday newspapers over the green grass for which the worthy men who do not work pay taxes. Then there is the "Hottest Sunday in the Park," which comes up a month later, when you increase the park policeman's former guess by fifteen thousand, and give it a news value by adding a list of the small boys drowned in bathing.

The "First Haul of Shad" in the Delaware is another reliable story, as is also the first ice fit for skating in the park; and then there is always the Thanksgiving story, when you ask the theatrical managers what they have to be thankful for, and have them tell you, "For the best season that this theatre has ever known, sir," and offer you a pass for two; and there is the New Year's story when you interview the local celebrities as to what they most want for the new year, and turn their commonplace replies into something clever. There is also a story on Christmas Day, and the one Conway had just written on the street scenes of Christmas Eve. After you have written one of these stories two or three times, you find it just as easy to write it in the office as anywhere else. One gentleman of my acquaintance did this most unsuccessfully. He wrote his Christmas-day story with the aid of a directory and the file of a last year's paper. From the year-old file he obtained the names of all the charitable institutions which made a practice of giving their charges presents and Christmas trees, and from the directory he drew the names of their presidents and boards of directors; but as he was unfortunately lacking in religious knowledge and a sense of humor, he included all the Jewish institutions on the list, and they wrote to the paper and rather objected to being represented as decorating Christmas trees, or in any way celebrating that particular day. But of all stale, flat, and unprofitable stories, this releasing of prisoners from Moyamensing was the worst. It seemed to Bronson that they were always releasing prisoners; he wondered how they possibly left themselves enough to make a county prison worth while. And the city editor for some reason always chose him to go down and see them come out. As they were released at midnight, and never did anything of moment when they were released but to immediately cross over to the nearest saloon with all their disreputable friends who had gathered to meet them, it was trying to one whose regard for the truth was at first unshaken, and whose imagination at the last became exhausted. So, when Bronson heard he had to release another prisoner in pathetic descriptive prose, he lost heart and patience, and rebelled.

"Andy," he said, sadly and impressively, "if I have written that story once, I have written it twenty times. I have described Moyamensing with the moonlight falling on its walls; I have described it with the walls shining in the rain; I have described it covered with the pure white snow that falls on the just as well as on the criminal; and I have made the bloodhounds in the jail-yard howl dismally—and there are no bloodhounds, as you very well know; and I have made released convicts declare their intention to lead a better and a purer life, when they only said, 'If youse put anything in the paper about me, I'll lay for you;' and I have made them fall on the necks of their weeping wives, when they only asked, 'Did you bring me some tobacco? I'm sick for a pipe;' and I will not write any more about it; and if I do, I will do it here in the office, and that is all there is to it."

"Oh yes, I think you will," said the city editor, easily.

"Let some one else do it," Bronson pleaded—"some one who hasn't done the thing to death, who will get a new point of view—" Conway, who had stopped writing, and had been grinning at Bronson over the city editor's back, grew suddenly grave and absorbed, and began to write again with feverish industry. "Conway, now, he's great at that sort of thing. He's—"

The city editor laid a clipping from the morning paper on the desk, and took a roll of bills from his pocket.

"There's the preliminary story," he said. "Conway wrote it, and it moved several good people to stop at the business office on their way down-town and leave something for the released convict's Christmas dinner. The story is a very good story, and impressed them," he went on, counting out the bills as he spoke, "to the extent of fifty five dollars. You take that and give it to him, and tell him to forget the past, and keep to the narrow road, and leave jointed jimmies alone. That money will give you an excuse for talking to him, and he may say something grateful to the paper, and comment on its enterprise. Come, now, get up. I've spoiled you two boys. You've been sulking all the evening because Conway got that story, and now you are sulking because you have got a better one. Think of it—getting out of prison after four years, and on Christmas Eve! It's a beautiful story just as it is. But," he added, grimly, "you'll try to improve on it, and grow maudlin. I believe sometimes you'd turn a red light on the dying gladiator."

The conscientiously industrious Conway, now that his fear of being sent out again was at rest, laughed at this with conciliatory mirth, and Bronson smiled sheepishly, and peace was restored between them.

But as Bronson capitulated, he tried to make conditions. "Can I take a cab?" he asked.

The city editor looked at his watch. "Yes," he said; "you'd better; it's late, and we go to press early to-night, remember."

"And can I send my stuff down by the driver and go home?" Bronson went on. "I can write it up there, and leave the cab at Fifteenth Street, near our house. I don't want to come all the way down-town again."

"No," said the chief; "the driver might lose it, or get drunk, or something."

"Then can I take Gallegher with me to bring it back?" asked Bronson. Gallegher was one of the office-boys.

The city editor stared at him grimly. "Wouldn't you like a type-writer, and Conway to write the story for you, and a hot supper sent after you?" he asked.

"No; Gallegher will do," Bronson said.

Gallegher had his overcoat on and a night-hawk at the door when Bronson came down the stairs and stopped to light a cigar in the hallway.

"Go to Moyamensing," said Gallegher to the driver.

Gallegher looked at the man to see if he would show himself sufficiently human to express surprise at their visiting such a place on such a night, but the man only gathered up his reins impassively, and Gallegher stepped into the cab, with a feeling of disappointment at having missed a point. He rubbed the frosted panes and looked out with boyish interest at the passing holiday-makers. The pavements were full of them and their bundles, and the street as well, with wavering lines of medical students and clerks blowing joyfully on the horns, and pushing through the crowd with one hand on the shoulder of the man in front. The Christmas greens hung in long lines, and only stopped where a street crossed, and the shop fronts were so brilliant that the street was as light as day.

It was so light that Bronson could read the clipping the city editor had given him.

"What is it we are going on?" asked Gallegher.

Gallegher enjoyed many privileges; they were given him principally, I think, because if they had not been given him he would have taken them. He was very young and small, but sturdily built, and he had a general knowledge which was entertaining, except when he happened to know more about anything than you did. It was impossible to force him to respect your years, for he knew all about you, from the number of lines that had been cut off your last story to the amount of your very small salary; and there was an awful simplicity about him, and a certain sympathy, or it may have been merely curiosity, which showed itself towards every one with whom he came in contact. So when he asked Bronson what he was going to do, Bronson read the clipping in his hand aloud.

"'Henry Quinn,'" Bronson read, "'who was sentenced to six years in Moyamensing Prison for the robbery of the Second National Bank at Tacony, will be liberated to-night. His sentence has been commuted, owing to good conduct and to the fact that for the last year he has been in very ill health. Quinn was night watchman at the Tacony bank at the time of the robbery, and, as was shown at the trial, was in reality merely the tool of the robbers. He confessed to complicity in the robbery, but disclaimed having any knowledge of the later whereabouts of the money, which has never been recovered. This was his first offence, and he had, up to the time of the robbery, borne a very excellent reputation. Although but lately married, his married life had been a most unhappy one, his friends claiming that his wife and her mother were the most to blame. Quinn took to spending his evenings away from home, and saw a great deal of a young woman who was supposed to have been the direct cause of his dishonesty. He admitted, in fact, that it was to get money to enable him to leave the country with her that he agreed to assist the bank-robbers. The paper acknowledges the receipt of ten dollars from M.J.C. to be given to Quinn on his release, also two dollars from Cash and three from Mary.'"

Gallegher's comment on this was one of disdain. "There isn't much in that," he said, "is there? Just a man that's done time once, and they're letting him out. Now, if it was Kid McCoy, or Billy Porter, or some one like that—eh?" Gallegher had as high a regard for a string of aliases after a name as others have for a double line of K.C.B.'s and C.S.L.'s, and a man who had offended but once was not worthy of his consideration. "And you will work in those bloodhounds again, too, I suppose," he said, gloomily.

The reporter pretended not to hear this, and to doze in the corner, and Gallegher whistled softly to himself and twisted luxuriously on the cushions. It was a half-hour later when Bronson awoke to find he had dozed in all seriousness, as a sudden current of cold air cut in his face, and he saw Gallegher standing with his hand on the open door, with the gray wall of the prison rising behind him.

Moyamensing looks like a prison. It is solidly, awfully suggestive of the sternness of its duty and of the hopelessness of its failing in it. It stands like a great fortress of the Middle Ages in a quadrangle of cheap brick and white dwelling-houses, and a few mean shops and tawdry saloons. It has the towers of a fortress, the pillars of an Egyptian temple; but more impressive than either of these is the awful simplicity of the bare, uncompromising wall that shuts out the prying eyes of the world and encloses those who are no longer of the world. It is hard to imagine what effect it has on those who remain in the houses about it. One would think they would sooner live overlooking a graveyard than such a place, with its mystery and hopelessness and unending silence, its hundreds of human inmates whom no one can see or hear, but who, one feels, are there.

Bronson, as he looked up at the prison, familiar as it was to him, admitted that he felt all this, by a frown and a slight shrug of the shoulders. "You are to wait here until twelve," he said to the driver of the nighthawk. "Don't go far away."

Bronson and the boy walked to an oyster-saloon that made one of the line of houses facing the gates of the prison on the opposite side of the street, and seated themselves at one of the tables from which Bronson could see out towards the northern entrance of the jail. He told Gallegher to eat something, so that the saloon-keeper would make them welcome and allow them to remain, and Gallegher climbed up on a high chair, and heard the man shout back his order to the kitchen with a faint smile of anticipation. It was eleven o'clock, but it was even then necessary to begin to watch, as there was a tradition in the office that prisoners with influence were sometimes released before their sentence was quite fulfilled, and Bronson eyed the "released prisoners' gate" from across the top of his paper. The electric lights before the prison showed every stone in its wall, and turned the icy pavements into black mirrors of light. On a church steeple a block away a round clock-face told the minutes, and Bronson wondered, if they dragged so slowly to him, how tardily they must follow one another to the men in the prison, who could not see the clock's face. The office-boy finished his supper, and went out to explore the neighborhood, and came back later to say that it was growing colder, and that he had found the driver in a saloon, but that he was, to all appearances, still sober. Bronson suggested that he had better sacrifice himself once again and eat something for the good of the house, and Gallegher assented listlessly, with the comment that one "might as well be eatin' as doin' nothin'." He went out again restlessly, and was gone for a quarter of an hour, and Bronson had re-read the day's paper and the signs on the wall and the clipping he had read before, and was thinking of going out to find him, when Gallegher put his head and arm through the door and beckoned to him from the outside. Bronson wrapped his coat up around his throat and followed him leisurely to the street. Gallegher halted at the curb, and pointed across to the figure of a woman pacing up and down in the glare of the electric lights, and making a conspicuous shadow on the white surface of the snow.

"That lady," said Gallegher, "asked me what door they let the released prisoners out of, an' I said I didn't know, but that I knew a young fellow who did."

Bronson stood considering the possible value of this for a moment, and then crossed the street slowly. The woman looked up sharply as he approached, but stood still.

"If you are waiting to see Quinn," Bronson said, abruptly, "he will come out of that upper gate, the green one with the iron spikes over it."

The woman stood motionless, and looked at him doubtfully. She was quite young and pretty, but her face was drawn and wearied-looking, as though she were a convalescent or one who was in trouble. She was of the working class.

"I am waiting for him myself," Bronson said, to reassure her.

"Are you?" the girl answered, vaguely. "Did you try to see him?" She did not wait for an answer, but went on, nervously: "They wouldn't let me see him. I have been here since noon. I thought maybe he might get out before that, and I'd be too late. You are sure that is the gate, are you? Some of them told me there was another, and I was afraid I'd miss him. I've waited so long," she added. Then she asked, "You're a friend of his, ain't you?"

"Yes, I suppose so," Bronson said. "I am waiting to give him some money."

"Yes? I have some money, too," the girl said, slowly. "Not much." Then she looked at Bronson eagerly and with a touch of suspicion, and took a step backward. "You're no friend of hern, are you?" she asked, sharply.

"Her? Whom do you mean?" asked Bronson.

But Gallegher interrupted him. "Certainly not," he said. "Of course not."

The girl gave a satisfied nod, and then turned to retrace her steps over the beat she had laid out for herself.

"Whom do you think she means?" asked Bronson, in a whisper.

"His wife, I suppose," Gallegher answered, impatiently.

The girl came back, as if finding some comfort in their presence. "*She's* inside now," with a nod of her head towards the prison. "Her and her mother. They come in a cab," she added, as if that circumstance made it a little harder to bear. "And when I asked if I could see him, the man at the gate said he had orders not. I suppose she gave him them orders. Don't you think so?" She did not wait for a reply, but went on as though she had been watching alone so long that it was a relief to speak to some one. "How much money have you got?" she asked.

Bronson told her.

"Fifty-five dollars!" The girl laughed, sadly. "I only got fifteen dollars. That ain't much, is it? That's all I could make—I've been sick—that and the fifteen I sent the paper."

"Was it you that—did you send any money to a paper?" asked Bronson.

"Yes; I sent fifteen dollars. I thought maybe I wouldn't get to speak to him if she came out with him, and I wanted him to have the money, so I sent it to the paper, and asked them to see he got it. I give it under three names: I give my initials, and 'Cash,' and just my name—— 'Mary.' I wanted him to know it was me give it. I suppose they'll send it all right. Fifteen dollars don't look like much against fifty-five dollars, does it?" She took a small roll of bills from her pocket and smiled down at them. Her hands were bare, and Bronson saw that they were chapped and rough. She rubbed them one over the other, and smiled at him wearily.

Bronson could not place her in the story he was about to write; it was a new and unlooked-for element, and one that promised to be of moment. He took the roll of bills from his pocket and handed them to her. "You might as well give him this too," he said. "I will be here until he comes out, and it makes no difference who gives him the money, so long as he gets it."

The girl smiled confusedly. The show of confidence seemed to please her. But she said, "No, I'd rather not. You see, it isn't mine, and I *did* work for this," holding out her own roll of money. She looked up at him steadily, and paused for a moment, and then said, almost defiantly, "Do you know who I am?"

"I can guess," Bronson said.

"Yes, I suppose you can," the girl answered. "Well, you can believe it or not, just as you please"—as though he had accused her of something—"but, before God, it wasn't my doings." She pointed with a wave of her hand towards the prison wall. "I did not know it was for *me* he helped them get the money until he said so on the stand. I didn't know he was thinking of running off with me at all. I guess I'd have gone if he had asked me. But I didn't put him up to it as they said I'd done. I knew he cared for me a lot, but I didn't think he cared as much as that. His wife"—she stopped, and seemed to consider her words carefully, as if to be quite fair in what she said—"his wife, I guess, didn't know just how to treat him. She was too fond of going out, and having company at the house, when he was away nights watching at the bank. When they was first married she used to go down to the bank and sit up with him to keep him company; but it was lonesome there in the dark, and she give it up. She was always fond of company and having men around. Her and her mother are a good deal alike. Henry used to grumble about it, and then she'd get mad, and that's how it begun. And then the neighbors talked too. It was after that that he got to coming to see me. I was living out in service then, and he used to stop in to see me on his way back from the bank, about seven in the morning, when I was up in the kitchen getting breakfast. I'd give him a cup of coffee or something, and that's how we got acquainted."

She turned her face away, and looked at the lights farther down the street. "They said a good deal about me and him that wasn't true." There was a pause, and then she looked at Bronson again. "I told him he ought to stop coming to see me, and to make it up with his wife, but he said he liked me best. I couldn't help his saying that, could I, if he did? Then he—then this come," she nodded to the jail, "and they blamed *me* for it. They said that I stood in with the bank-robbers, and was working with them; they said they used me for to get him to help them." She lifted her face to the boy and the man, and they saw that her eyes were wet and that her face was quivering. "That's likely, isn't it?" she demanded, with a sob. She stood for a moment looking at the great iron gate, and then at the clock-face glowing dully through the falling snow: it showed a quarter to twelve. "When he was put away," she went on, sadly, "I started in to wait for him, and to save something against his coming out. I only got three dollars a week and my keep, but I had saved one hundred and thirty dollars up to last April, and then I took sick, and it all went to the doctor and for medicines. I didn't want to spend it that way, but I couldn't die and not see him. Sometimes I thought it would be better if I did die and save the money for him, and then there wouldn't be any more trouble, anyway. But I couldn't make up my mind to do it. I did go without taking medicines they laid out for me for three days; but I had to live—I just *had* to. Sometimes I think I ought to have given up, and not tried to get well. What do you think?"

Bronson shook his head, and cleared his throat as if he were going to speak, but said nothing. Gallegher was looking up at the girl with large, open eyes. Bronson wondered if any woman would ever love him as much as that, or if he would ever love any woman so. It made him feel lonesome, and he shook his head. "Well?" he said, impatiently.

"Well, that's all; that's how it is," she said. "She's been living on there at Tacony with her mother. She kept seeing as many men as before, and kept getting pitied all the time; everybody was so sorry for her. When he was took so bad that time a year ago with his lungs, they said in Tacony that if he died she'd marry Charley Oakes, the conductor. He's always going to see her. Them that knew her knew me, and I got word about how Henry was getting on. I couldn't see him, because she told lies about me to the warden, and they wouldn't let me. But I got word about him. He's been fearful sick just lately. He caught a cold walking in the yard, and it got down to his lungs. That's why they are letting him out. They say he's changed so. I wonder if I'm changed much?" she said. "I've fallen off since I was ill." She passed her hands slowly over her face, with a touch of vanity that hurt Bronson somehow, and he wished he might tell her how pretty she still was. "Do you think he'll know me?" she asked. "Do you think she'll let me speak to him?"

"I don't know. How can I tell?" said the reporter, sharply. He was strangely nervous and upset. He could see no way out of it. The girl seemed to be telling the truth, and yet the man's wife was with him and by his side, as she should be, and this woman had no place on the scene, and could mean nothing but trouble to herself and to every one else. "Come," he said, abruptly, "we had better be getting up there. It's only five minutes of twelve."

The girl turned with a quick start, and walked on ahead of them up the drive leading between the snow-covered grass-plots that stretched from the pavement to the wall of the prison. She moved unsteadily and slowly, and Bronson saw that she was shivering, either from excitement or the cold.

"I guess," said Gallegher, in an awed whisper, "that there's going to be a scrap."

"Shut up," said Bronson.

They stopped a few yards before the great green double gate, with a smaller door cut in one of its halves, and with the light from a big lantern shining down on them. They could not see the clock-face from where they stood, and when Bronson took out his watch and looked at it, the girl turned her face to his appealingly, but did not speak.

"It will be only a little while now," he said, gently. He thought he had never seen so much trouble and fear and anxiety in so young a face, and he moved towards her and said, in a whisper, as though those inside could hear him, "Control yourself if you can," and then added, doubtfully, and still in a whisper, "You can take my arm if you need it." The girl shook her head dumbly, but took a step nearer him, as if for protection, and turned her eyes fearfully towards the gate. The minutes passed on slowly but with intense significance, and they stood so still that they could hear the wind playing through the wires of the electric light back of them, and the clicking of the icicles as they dropped from the edge of the prison wall to the stones at their feet.

And then slowly and laboriously, and like a knell, the great gong of the prison sounded the first stroke of twelve; but before it had counted three there came suddenly from all the city about them a great chorus of clanging bells and the shrieks and tooting of whistles and the booming of cannon. From far down town the big bell of the State-house, with its prestige and historic dignity back of it, tried to give the time, but the other bells raced past it, and beat out on the cold crisp air joyously and uproariously from Kensington to the Schuylkill; and from far across the Neck, over the marshes and frozen ponds, came the dull roar of the guns at the navy-yard, and from the Delaware the hoarse tootings of the ferry-boats, and the sharp shrieks of the tugs, until the heavens seemed to rock and swing with the great welcome.

Gallegher looked up quickly with a queer, awed smile.

"It's Christmas," he said, and then he nodded doubtfully towards Bronson and said, "Merry Christmas, sir."

It had come to the waiting holiday crowd down-town around the State-house, to the captain of the tug, fog-bound on the river, to the engineer sweeping across the white fields and sounding his welcome with his hand on the bell-cord, to the prisoners beyond the walls, and to the children all over the land, watching their stockings at the foot of their beds.

And then the three were instantly drawn down to earth again by the near, sharp click of opening bolts and locks, and the green gates swung heavily in before them. The jail-yard was light with whitewash, and two great lamps in front of round reflectors shone with blinding force in their faces, and made them start suddenly backward, as though they had been caught in the act and held in the circle of a policeman's lantern. In the middle of the yard was the carriage in which the prisoner's wife and her mother had come, and around it stood the wardens and turnkeys in their blue and gold uniforms. They saw them, dimly from behind the glare of the carriage lamps that shone in their faces, and saw the horses moving slowly towards them, and the driver holding up their heads as they slipped and slid on the icy stones. The girl put her hand on Bronson's arm and clinched it with her fingers, but her eyes were on the advancing carriage. The horses slipped nearer to them and passed them, and the lights from the lamps now showed their backs and the paving stones beyond them, and left the cab in partial darkness. It was a four-seated carriage with a movable top, opening into two halves at the centre. It had been closed when the cab first entered the prison, a few hours before, but now its top was thrown back, and they could see that it held the two women, who sat facing each other on the farther side, and on the side nearer them, stretching from the forward seat to the top of the back, was a plain board coffin, prison-made and painted black.

The girl at Bronson's side gave something between a cry and a shriek that turned him sick for an instant, and that made the office-boy drop his head between his shoulders as though some one had struck at him from above. Even the horses shied with sudden panic towards one another, and the driver pulled them in with an oath of consternation, and threw himself forward to look beneath their hoofs. And as the carriage stopped the girl sprang in between the wheels and threw her arms across the lid of the coffin, and laid her face down upon the boards that were already damp with the falling snow.

"Henry! Henry! Henry!" she moaned.

The surgeon who attended the prisoner through the sickness that had cheated the country of three hours of his sentence ran out from the hurrying crowd of wardens and drew the girl slowly and gently away, and the two women moved on triumphantly with their sorry victory.

Bronson gave his copy to Gallegher to take to the office, and Gallegher laid it and the roll of money on the city editor's desk, and then, so the chief related afterwards, moved off quickly to the door. The chief looked up from his proofs and touched the roll of money with his pencil. "Here! what's this?" he asked. "Wouldn't he take it?"

Gallegher stopped and straightened himself as though about to tell with proper dramatic effect the story of the night's adventure, and then, as though the awe of it still hung upon him, backed slowly to the door, and said, confusedly, "No, sir; he was—he didn't need it."

AN UNFINISHED STORY

Mrs. Trevelyan, as she took her seat, shot a quick glance down the length of her table and at the arrangement of her guests, and tried to learn if her lord and master approved. But he was listening to something Lady Arbuthnot, who sat on his right, was saying, and, being a man, failed to catch her meaning, and only smiled unconcernedly and cheerfully back at her. But the wife of the Austrian Minister, who was her very dearest friend, saw and appreciated, and gave her a quick little smile over her fan, which said that the table was perfect, the people most interesting, and that she could possess her soul in peace. So Mrs. Trevelyan pulled at the tips of her gloves and smiled upon her guests. Mrs. Trevelyan was not used to questioning her powers, but this dinner had been almost impromptu, and she had been in doubt. It was quite unnecessary, for her dinner carried with it the added virtue of being the last of the season, an encore to all that had gone before—a special number by request on the social programme. It was not one of many others stretching on for weeks, for the summer's change and leisure began on the morrow, and there was nothing hanging over her guests that they must go on to later. They knew that their luggage stood ready locked and strapped at home; they could look before them to the whole summer's pleasure, and they were relaxed and ready to be pleased, and broke simultaneously into a low murmur of talk and laughter. The windows of the dining-room stood open from the floor, and from the tiny garden that surrounded the house, even in the great mass of stucco and brick of encircling London, came the odor of flowers and of fresh turf. A soft summer-night wind moved the candles under their red shades; and gently as though they rose from afar, and not only from across the top of the high wall before the house, came the rumble of the omnibuses passing farther into the suburbs, and the occasional quick rush of a hansom over the smooth asphalt. It was a most delightful choice of people, gathered at short notice and to do honor to no one in particular, but to give each a chance to say good-by before he or she met the yacht at Southampton or took the club train to Homburg. They all knew each other very well; and if there was a guest of the evening, it was one of the two Americans—either Miss Egerton, the girl who was to marry Lord Arbuthnot, whose mother sat on Trevelyan's right, or young Gordon, the explorer, who has just come out of Africa. Miss Egerton was a most strikingly beautiful girl, with a strong, fine face, and an earnest, interested way when she spoke, which the English found most attractive. In appearance she had been variously likened by Trevelyan, who was painting her portrait, to a druidess, a vestal virgin, and a Greek goddess; and Lady Arbuthnot's friends, who thought to please the girl, assured her that no one would ever suppose her to be an American—their ideas of the

American young woman having been gathered from those who pick out tunes with one finger on the pianos in the public parlors of the Métropole. Miss Egerton was said to be intensely interested in her lover's career, and was as ambitious for his success in the House as he was himself. They were both very much in love, and showed it to others as little as people of their class do. The others at the table were General Sir Henry Kent; Phillips, the novelist; the Austrian Minister and his young wife; and Trevelyan, who painted portraits for large sums of money and figure pieces for art; and some simply fashionable smart people who were good listeners, and who were rather disappointed that the American explorer was no more sun-burned than other young men who had stayed at home, and who had gone in for tennis or yachting.

The worst of Gordon was that he made it next to impossible for one to lionize him. He had been back in civilization and London only two weeks, unless Cairo and Shepheard's Hotel are civilization, and he had been asked everywhere, and for the first week had gone everywhere. But whenever his hostess looked for him, to present another and not so recent a lion, he was generally found either humbly carrying an ice to some neglected dowager, or talking big game or international yachting or tailors to a circle of younger sons in the smoking-room, just as though several hundred attractive and distinguished people were not waiting to fling the speeches they had prepared on Africa at him, in the drawing-room above. He had suddenly disappeared during the second week of his stay in London, which was also the last week of the London season, and managers of lecture tours and publishers and lion-hunters, and even friends who cared for him for himself, had failed to find him at his lodgings. Trevelyan, who had known him when he was a travelling correspondent and artist for one of the great weeklies, had found him at the club the night before, and had asked him to his wife's impromptu dinner, from which he had at first begged off, but, on learning who was to be there, had changed his mind and accepted. Mrs. Trevelyan was very glad he had come; she had always spoken of him as a nice boy, and now that he had become famous she liked him none the less, but did not show it before people as much as she had been used to do. She forgot to ask him whether he knew his beautiful compatriot or not; but she took it for granted that they had met, if not at home, at least in London, as they had both been made so much of, and at the same houses.

The dinner was well on its way towards its end, and the women had begun to talk across the table, and to exchange bankers' addresses, and to say "Be sure and look us up in Paris," and "When do you expect to sail from Cowes?" They were enlivened and interested, and the present odors of the food and flowers and wine, and the sense of leisure before them, made it seem almost a pity that such a well-suited gathering should have to separate for even a summer's pleasure.

The Austrian Minister was saying this to his hostess, when Sir Henry Kent, who had been talking across to Phillips, the novelist, leaned back in his place and said, as though to challenge the attention of every one, "I can't agree with you, Phillips. I am sure no one else will."

"Dear me," complained Mrs. Trevelyan, plaintively, "what have you been saying now, Mr. Phillips? He always has such debatable theories," she explained.

"On the contrary, Mrs. Trevelyan," answered the novelist, "it is the other way. It is Sir Henry who is making all the trouble. He is attacking one of the oldest and dearest platitudes I know." He paused for the general to speak, but the older man nodded his head for him to go on. "He has just said that fiction is stranger than truth," continued the novelist. "He says that I—that people who write could never interest people who read if they wrote of things as they really are. They select, he says—they take the critical moment in a man's life and the crises, and want others to believe that that is what happens every day. Which it is not, so the general says. He thinks that life is commonplace and uneventful—that is, uneventful in a picturesque or dramatic way. He admits that women's lives are saved from drowning, but that they are not saved by their lovers, but by a longshoreman with a wife and six children, who accepts five pounds for doing it. That's it, is it not?" he asked.

The general nodded and smiled. "What I said to Phillips was," he explained, "that if things were related just as they happen, they would not be interesting. People do not say the dramatic things they say on the stage or in novels; in real life they are commonplace or sordid—or disappointing. I have seen men die on the battle-field, for instance, and they never cried, 'I die that my country may live,' or 'I have got my promotion at last;' they just stared up at the surgeon and said, 'Have I got to lose that arm?' or 'I am killed, I think.' You see, when men are dying around you, and horses are plunging, and the batteries are firing, one doesn't have time to think up the appropriate remark for the occasion. I don't believe, now, that Pitt's last words were, 'Roll up the map of Europe.' A man who could change the face of a continent would not use his dying breath in making epigrams. It was one of his secretaries or one of the doctors who said that. And the man who was capable of writing home, 'All is lost but honor,' was just the sort of a man who would lose more battles than he would win. No; you, Phillips," said the general, raising his voice as he became more confident and conscious that be held the centre of the stage, "and you, Trevelyan, don't write and paint every-day things as they are. You introduce something for a contrast or for an effect; a red coat in a landscape for the bit of color you want, when in real life the red coat would not be within miles; or you have a band of music playing a popular air in the street when a murder is going on inside the house. You do it because it is effective; but it isn't true. Now Mr. Caithness was telling us the other night at the club, on this very matter—"

"Oh, that's hardly fair," laughed Trevelyan; "you've rehearsed all this before. You've come prepared."

"No, not at all," frowned the general, sweeping on. "He said that before he was raised to the bench, when he practised criminal law, he had brought word to a man that he was to be reprieved, and to another that he was to die. Now, you know," exclaimed the general, with a shrug, and appealing to the table, "how that would be done on the stage or in a novel, with the prisoner bound ready for execution, and a galloping horse, and a fluttering piece of white paper, and all that. Well, now, Caithness told us that he went into the man's cell and said, 'You have been reprieved, John,' or William, or whatever the fellow's name was. And the man looked at him and said: 'Is that so? That's good—that's good;' and that was all he said. And then, again, he told one man whose life he had tried very hard to save: 'The Home Secretary has refused to intercede for you. I saw him at his house last night at nine o'clock.' And the murderer, instead of saying, 'My God! what will my wife and children do?' looked at him, and repeated, 'At nine o'clock last night!' just as though that were the important part of the message."

"Well, but, general," said Phillips, smiling, "that's dramatic enough as it is, I think. Why—"

"Yes," interrupted the general, quickly and triumphantly. "But that is not what you would have made him say, is it? That's my point."

"There was a man told me once," Lord Arbuthnot began, leisurely—"he was a great chum of mine, and it illustrates what Sir Henry has said, I think—he was engaged to a girl, and he had a misunderstanding or an understanding with her that opened both their eyes, at a dance, and the next afternoon he called, and they talked it over in the drawing-room, with the tea-tray between them, and agreed to end it. On the stage he would have risen and said, 'Well, the comedy is over, the tragedy begins, or the curtain falls;' and she would have gone to the piano and played Chopin sadly while he made his exit. Instead of which he got up to go without saying anything, and as he rose he upset a cup and saucer on the tea-table, and said, 'Oh, I beg your pardon;' and she said, 'It isn't broken;' and he went out. You see," the young man added, smiling, "there were two young people whose hearts were breaking, and yet they talked of teacups, not because they did not feel, but because custom is too strong on us and too much for us. We do not say dramatic things or do theatrical ones. It does not make interesting reading, but it is the truth."

"Exactly," cut in the Austrian Minister, eagerly. "And then there is the prerogative of the author and of the playwright to drop a curtain whenever he wants to, or to put a stop to everything by ending the chapter. That isn't fair. That is an advantage over nature. When some one accuses some one else of doing something dreadful at the play, down comes the curtain quick and keeps things at fever point, or the chapter ends with a lot of stars, and the next page begins with a description of a sunset two weeks later. To be true, we ought to be told what the man who is accused said in the reply, or what happened during those two weeks before the sunset. The author really has no right to choose only the critical moments, and to shut out the commonplace, every-day life by a sort of literary closure. That is, if he claims to tell the truth."

Phillips raised his eyebrows and looked carefully around the table. "Does any one else feel called upon to testify?" he asked.

"It's awful, isn't it, Phillips," laughed Trevelyan, comfortably, "to find that the photographer is the only artist, after all? I feel very guilty."

"You ought to," pronounced the general, gayly. He was very well satisfied with himself at having held his own against these clever people. "And I am sure Mr. Gordon will agree with me, too," he went on, confidently, with a bow towards the younger man. "He has seen more of the world than any of us, and he will tell you, I am sure, that what happens only suggests the story; it is not complete in itself. That it always needs the author's touch, just as the rough diamond—"

"Oh, thanks, thanks, general," laughed Phillips. "My feelings are not hurt as badly as that."

Gordon had been turning the stem of a wineglass slowly between his thumb and his finger while the others were talking, and looking down at it smiling. Now he raised his eyes as though he meant to speak, and then dropped them again. "I am afraid, Sir Henry," he said, "that I don't agree with you at all."

Those who had said nothing felt a certain satisfaction that they had not committed themselves. The Austrian Minister tried to remember what it was he had said, and whether it was too late to retreat, and the general looked blankly at Gordon and said, "Indeed?"

"You shouldn't have called on that last witness, Sir Henry," said Phillips, smiling. "Your case was very good as it was."

"I am quite sure," said Gordon, seriously, "that the story Phillips will never write is a true story, but he will not write it because people would say it is impossible, just as you have all seen sunsets sometimes that you knew would be laughed at if any one tried to paint them. We all know such a story, something in our own lives, or in the lives of our friends. Not ghost stories, or stories of adventure, but of ambitions that come to nothing, of people who were rewarded or punished in this world instead of in the next, and love stories."

Phillips looked at the young man keenly and smiled. "Especially love stories," he said.

Gordon looked back at him as if he did not understand.

"Tell it, Gordon," said Mr. Trevelyan.

"Yes," said Gordon, nodding his head in assent, "I was thinking of a particular story. It is as complete, I think, and as dramatic as any of those we read. It is about a man I met in Africa. It is not a long story," he said, looking around the table tentatively, "but it ends badly."

There was a silence much more appreciated than a polite murmur of invitation would have been, and the simply smart people settled themselves rigidly to catch every word for future use. They realized that this would be a story which had not as yet appeared in the newspapers, and which would not make a part of Gordon's book. Mrs. Trevelyan smiled encouragingly upon her former protégé; she was sure he was going to do himself credit; but the American girl chose this chance, when all the other eyes were turned expectantly towards the explorer, to look at her lover.

"We were on our return march from Lake Tchad to the Mobangi," said Gordon. "We had been travelling over a month, sometimes by water and sometimes through the forest, and we did not expect to see any other white men besides those of our own party for several months to come. In the middle of a jungle late one afternoon I found this man lying at the foot of a tree. He had been cut and beaten and left for dead. It was as much of a surprise to me, you understand, as it would be to you if you were driving through Trafalgar Square in a hansom, and an African lion should spring up on your horses' haunches. We believed we were the only white men that had ever succeeded in getting that far south. Crampel had tried it, and no one knows yet whether he is dead or alive; Doctor Schlemen had been eaten by cannibals, and Major Bethume had turned back two hundred miles farther north; and we could no more account for this man's presence than if he had been dropped from the clouds. Lieutenant Royce, my surgeon, went to work at him, and we halted where we were for the night. In about an hour the man moved and opened his eyes. He looked up at us and said, 'Thank God!'—because we were white, I suppose—and went off into unconsciousness again. When he came to the next time, he asked Royce, in a whisper, how long he had to live. He wasn't the sort of a man you had to lie to about a thing like that, and Royce told him he did not think he could live for more than an hour or two. The man moved his head to show that he understood, and raised his hand to his throat and began pulling at his shirt, but the effort sent him off into a fainting-fit again. I opened his collar for him as gently as I could, and found that his fingers had clinched around a silver necklace that he wore about his neck, and from which there hung a gold locket shaped like a heart."

Gordon raised his eyes slowly from the observation of his finger-tips as they rested on the edge of the table before him to those of the American girl who sat opposite. She had heard his story so far without any show of attention, and had been watching, rather with a touch of fondness in her eyes, the clever, earnest face of Arbuthnot, who was following Gordon's story with polite interest. But now, at Gordon's last words, she turned her eyes to him with a look of awful indignation, which was followed, when she met his calmly polite look of inquiry, by one of fear and almost of entreaty.

"When the man came to," continued Gordon, in the same conventional monotone, "he begged me to take the chain and locket to a girl whom he said I would find either in London or in New York. He gave me the address of her banker. He said: 'Take it off my neck before you bury me; tell her I wore it ever since she gave it to me. That it has been a charm and loadstone to me. That when the locket rose and fell against my breast, it was as if her heart were pressing against mine and answering the beating and throbbing of the blood in my veins.'"

Gordon paused, and returned to the thoughtful scrutiny of his finger-tips.

"The man did not die," he said, raising his head. "Royce brought him back into such form again that in about a week we were able to take him along with us on a litter. But he was very weak, and would lie for hours sleeping when we rested, or mumbling and raving in a fever. We learned from him at odd times that he had been trying to reach Lake Tchad, to do what we had done, without any means of doing it. He had had not more than a couple of dozen porters and a corporal's guard of Senegalese soldiers. He was the only white man in the party, and his men had turned on him, and left him as we found him, carrying off with them his stock of provisions and arms. He had undertaken the expedition on a promise from the French government to make him governor of the territory he opened up if he succeeded, but he had had no official help. If he failed, he got nothing; if he succeeded, he did so at his own expense and by his own endeavors. It was only a wonder he had been able to get as far as he did. He did not seem to feel the failure of his expedition. All that was lost in the happiness of getting back alive to this woman with whom he was in love. He had been three days alone before we found him, and in those three days, while he waited for death, he had thought of nothing but that he would never see her again. He had resigned himself to this, had given up all hope, and our coming seemed like a miracle to him. I have read about men in love, I have seen it on the stage, I have seen it in real life, but I never saw a man so grateful to God and so happy and so insane over a woman as this man was. He raved about her when he was feverish, and he talked and talked to me about her when he was in his senses. The porters could not understand him, and he found me sympathetic, I suppose, or else he did not care, and only wanted to speak of her to some one, and so he told me the story over and over again as I walked beside the litter, or as we sat by the fire at night. She must have been a very remarkable girl. He had met her first the year before, on one of the Italian steamers that ply from New York to Gibraltar. She was travelling with her father, who was an invalid going to Tangier for his health; from Tangier they were to go on up to Nice and Cannes, and in the spring to Paris and on to London for this season just over. The man was going from Gibraltar to Zanzibar, and then on into the Congo. They had met the first night out; they had separated thirteen days later at Gibraltar, and in that time the girl had fallen in love with him, and had promised to marry him if he would let her, for he was very proud. He had to be. He had absolutely nothing to offer her. She is very well known at home. I mean her family is: they have lived in New York from its first days, and they are very rich. The girl had lived a life as different from his as the life of a girl in society must be from that of a vagabond. He had been an engineer, a newspaper correspondent, an officer in a Chinese army, and had built bridges in South America, and led their little revolutions there, and had seen service on the desert in the French army of Algiers. He had no home or nationality even, for he had left America when he was sixteen; he had no family, had saved no money, and was trusting everything to the success of this expedition into Africa to make him known and to give him position. It was the story of Othello and Desdemona over again. His blackness lay from her point of view, or rather would have lain from the point of view of her friends, in the fact that he was as helplessly ineligible a young man as a cowboy. And he really had lived a life of which he had no great reason to be proud. He had existed entirely for excitement, as other men live to drink until they kill themselves by it; nothing he had done had counted for much except his bridges. They are still standing. But the things he had written are lost in the columns of the daily papers. The soldiers he had fought with knew him only as a man who cared more for the fighting than for what the fighting was about, and he had been as ready to write on one side as to fight on the other. He was a rolling stone, and had been a rolling stone from the time he was sixteen and had run away to sea, up to the day he had met this girl, when he was just thirty. Yet you can see how such a man would attract a young, impressionable girl, who had met only those men whose actions are bounded by the courts of law or Wall Street, or the younger set who drive coaches and who live the life of the clubs. She had gone through life as some people go through picture-galleries, with their catalogues marked at the best pictures.

She knew nothing of the little fellows whose work was skied, who were trying to be known, who were not of her world, but who toiled and prayed and hoped to be famous. This man came into her life suddenly with his stories of adventure and strange people and strange places, of things done for the love of doing them and not for the reward or reputation, and he bewildered her at first, I suppose, and then fascinated, and then won her. You can imagine how it was, these two walking the deck together during the day, or sitting side by side when the night came on, the ocean stretched before them. The daring of his present undertaking, the absurd glamour that is thrown over those who have gone into that strange country from which some travellers return, and the picturesqueness of his past life. It is no wonder the girl made too much of him. I do not think he knew what was coming. He did not pose before her. I am quite sure, from what I knew of him, that he did not. Indeed, I believed him when he said that he had fought against the more than interest she had begun to show for him. He was the sort of man women care for, but they had not been of this woman's class or calibre. It came to him like a sign from the heavens. It was as if a goddess had stooped to him. He told her when they separated that if he succeeded—if he opened this unknown country, if he was rewarded as they had promised to reward him—he might dare to come to her; and she called him her knight-errant, and gave him her chain and locket to wear, and told him, whether he failed or succeeded it meant nothing to her, and that her life was his while it lasted, and her soul as well.

"I think," Gordon said, stopping abruptly, with an air of careful consideration, "that those were her words as he repeated them to me."

He raised his eyes thoughtfully towards the face of the girl opposite, and then glanced past her, as if he were trying to recall the words the man had used. The fine, beautiful face of the woman was white and drawn around the lips, and she gave a quick, appealing glance at her hostess, as if she would beg to be allowed to go. But Mrs. Trevelyan and her guests were watching Gordon or toying with the things in front of them. The dinner had been served, and not even the soft movements of the servants interrupted the young man's story.

"You can imagine a man," Gordon went on, more lightly, "finding a hansom cab slow when he is riding from the station to see the woman he loves; but imagine this man urging himself and the rest of us to hurry when we were in the heart of Africa, with six months' travel in front of us before we could reach the first limits of civilization. That is what this man did. When he was still on his litter he used to toss and turn, and abuse the bearers and porters and myself because we moved so slowly. When we stopped for the night he would chafe and fret at the delay; and when the morning came he was the first to wake, if he slept at all, and eager to push on. When at last he was able to walk, he worked himself into a fever again, and it was only when Royce warned him that he would kill himself if he kept on that he submitted to be carried, and forced himself to be patient. And all the time the poor devil kept saying how unworthy he was of her, how miserably he had wasted his years, how unfitted he was for the great happiness which had come into his life. I suppose every man says that when he is in love; very properly, too; but the worst of it was, in this man's case, that it was so very true. He was unworthy of her in everything but his love for her. It used to frighten me to see how much he cared. Well, we got out of it at last, and reached Alexandria, and saw white faces once more, and heard women's voices, and the strain and fear of failure were over, and we could breathe again. I was quite ready enough to push on to London, but we had to wait a week for the steamer, and during that time that man made my life miserable. He had done so well, and would have done so much more if he had had my equipment, that I tried to see that he received all the credit due him. But he would have none of the public receptions, and the audience with the khedive, or any of the fuss they made over us. He only wanted to get back to her. He spent the days on the quay watching them load the steamer, and counting the hours until she was to sail; and even at night he would leave the first bed he had slept in for six months, and would come into my room and ask me if I would not sit up and talk with him until daylight. You see, after he had given up all thought of her, and believed himself about to die without seeing her again, it made her all the dearer, I suppose, and made him all the more fearful of losing her again.

"He became very quiet as soon as we were really under way, and Royce and I hardly knew him for the same man. He would sit in silence in his steamer-chair for hours, looking out at the sea and smiling to himself, and sometimes, for he was still very weak and feverish, the tears would come to his eyes and run down his cheeks. 'This is the way we would sit,' he said to me one night, 'with the dark purple sky and the strange Southern stars over our heads, and the rail of the boat rising and sinking below the line of the horizon. And I can hear her voice, and I try to imagine she is still sitting there, as she did the last night out, when I held her hands between mine.'" Gordon paused a moment, and then went on more slowly: "I do not know whether it was that the excitement of the journey overland had kept him up or not, but as we went on he became much weaker and slept more, until Royce became anxious and alarmed about him. But he did not know it himself; he had grown so sure of his recovery then that he did not understand what the weakness meant. He fell off into long spells of sleep or unconsciousness, and woke only to be fed, and would then fall back to sleep again. And in one of these spells of unconsciousness he died. He died within two days of land. He had no home and no country and no family, as I told you, and we buried him at sea. He left nothing behind him, for the very clothes he wore were those we had given him—nothing but the locket and the chain which he had told me to take from his neck when he died."

Gordon's voice had grown very cold and hard. He stopped and ran his fingers down into his pocket and pulled out a little leather bag. The people at the table watched him in silence as he opened it and took out a dull silver chain with a gold heart hanging from it.

"This is it," he said, gently. He leaned across the table, with his eyes fixed on those of the American girl, and dropped the chain in front of her. "Would you like to see it?" he said.

The rest moved curiously forward to look at the little heap of gold and silver as it lay on the white cloth. But the girl, with her eyes half closed and her lips pressed together, pushed it on with her hand to the man who sat next her, and bowed her head slightly, as though it was an effort for her to move at all. The wife of the Austrian Minister gave a little sigh of relief.

"I should say your story did end badly, Mr. Gordon," she said. "It is terribly sad, and so unnecessarily so."

"I don't know," said Lady Arbuthnot, thoughtfully—"I don't know; it seems to me it was better. As Mr. Gordon says, the man was hardly worthy of her. A man should have something more to offer a woman than love; it is a woman's prerogative to be loved. Any number of men may love her; it is nothing to their credit: they cannot help themselves."

"Well," said General Kent, "if all true stories turn out as badly as that one does, I will take back what I said against those the story-writers tell. I prefer the ones Anstey and Jerome make up. I call it a most unpleasant story."

"But it isn't finished yet," said Gordon, as he leaned over and picked up the chain and locket. "There is still a little more."

"Oh, I beg your pardon!" said the wife of the Austrian Minister, eagerly. "But then," she added, "you can't make it any better. You cannot bring the man back to life."

"No," said Gordon, "but I can make it a little worse."

"Ah, I see," said Phillips, with a story-teller's intuition—"the girl."

"The first day I reached London I went to her banker's and got her address," continued Gordon. "And I wrote, saying I wanted to see her, but before I could get an answer I met her the next afternoon at a garden-party. At least I did not meet her; she was pointed out to me. I saw a very beautiful girl surrounded by a lot of men, and asked who she was, and found out it was the woman I had written to, the owner of the chain and locket; and I was also told that her engagement had just been announced to a young

Englishman of family and position, who had known her only a few months, and with whom she was very much in love. So you see," he went on, smiling, "that it was better that he died, believing in her and in her love for him. Mr. Phillips, now, would have let him live to return and find her married; but Nature is kinder than writers of fiction, and quite as dramatic."

Phillips did not reply to this, and the general only shook his head doubtfully and said nothing. So Mrs. Trevelyan looked at Lady Arbuthnot, and the ladies rose and left the room. When the men had left them, a young girl went to the piano, and the other women seated themselves to listen; but Miss Egerton, saying that it was warm, stepped out through one of the high windows on to the little balcony that overhung the garden. It was dark out there and cool, and the rumbling of the encircling city sounded as distant and as far off as the reflection seemed that its million lights threw up to the sky above. The girl leaned her face and bare shoulder against the rough stone wall of the house, and pressed her hands together, with her fingers locking and unlocking and her rings cutting through her gloves. She was trembling slightly, and the blood in her veins was hot and tingling. She heard the voices of the men as they entered the drawing-room, the momentary cessation of the music at the piano, and its renewal, and then a figure blocked the light from the window, and Gordon stepped out of it and stood in front of her with the chain and locket in his hand. He held it towards her, and they faced each other for a moment in silence.

"Will you take it now?" he said.

The girl raised her head, and drew herself up until she stood straight and tall before him. "Have you not punished me enough?" she asked, in a whisper. "Are you not satisfied? Was it brave? Was it manly? Is that what you have learned among your savages—to torture a woman?" She stopped with a quick sob of pain, and pressed her hands against her breast.

Gordon observed her, curiously, with cold consideration. "What of the sufferings of the man to whom you gave this?" he asked. "Why not consider him? What was your bad quarter of an hour at the table, with your friends around you, to the year he suffered danger and physical pain for you—for you, remember?"

The girl hid her face for a moment in her hands, and when she lowered them again her cheeks were wet and her voice was changed and softer. "They told me he was dead," she said. "Then it was denied, and then the French papers told of it again, and with horrible detail, and how it happened."

Gordon took a step nearer her. "And does your love come and go with the editions of the daily papers?" he asked, fiercely. "If they say to-morrow morning that Arbuthnot is false to his principles or his party, that he is a bribe-taker, a man who sells his vote, will you believe them and stop loving him?" He gave a sharp exclamation of disdain. "Or will you wait," he went on, bitterly, "until the Liberal organs have had time to deny it? Is that the love, the life, and the soul you promised the man who—"

There was a soft step on the floor of the drawing-room, and the tall figure of young Arbuthnot appeared in the opening of the window as he looked doubtfully out into the darkness. Gordon took a step back into the light of the window, where he could be seen, and leaned easily against the railing of the balcony. His eyes were turned towards the street, and he noticed over the wall the top of a passing omnibus and the glow of the men's pipes who sat on it.

"Miss Egerton?" asked Arbuthnot, his eyes still blinded by the lights of the room he had left. "Is she here? Oh, is that you?" he said, as he saw the movement of the white dress. "I was sent to look for you," he said. "They were afraid something was wrong." He turned to Gordon, as if in explanation of his lover-like solicitude. "It has been rather a hard week, and it has kept one pretty well on the go all the time, and I thought Miss Egerton looked tired at dinner."

The moment he had spoken, the girl came towards him quickly, and put her arm inside of his, and took his hand.

He looked down at her wonderingly at this show of affection, and then drew her nearer, and said, gently, "You are tired, aren't you? I came to tell you that Lady Arbuthnot is going. She is waiting for you."

It struck Gordon, as they stood there, how handsome they were and how well suited. They took a step towards the window, and then the young nobleman turned and looked out at the pretty garden and up at the sky, where the moon was struggling against the glare of the city.

"It is very pretty and peaceful out here," he said, "is it not? It seems a pity to leave it. Good-night, Gordon, and thank you for your story." He stopped, with one foot on the threshold, and smiled. "And yet, do you know," he said, "I cannot help thinking you were guilty of doing just what you accused Phillips of doing. I somehow thought you helped the true story out a little. Now didn't you? Was it all just as you told it? Or am I wrong?"

"No," Gordon answered; "you are right. I did change it a little, in one particular."

"And what was that, may I ask?" said Arbuthnot.

"The man did not die," Gordon answered.

Arbuthnot gave a quick little sigh of sympathy. "Poor devil!" he said, softly; "poor chap!" He moved his left hand over and touched the hand of the girl, as though to reassure himself of his own good fortune. Then he raised his eyes to Gordon's with a curious, puzzled look in them. "But then," he said, doubtfully, "if he is not dead, how did you come to get the chain?"

The girl's arm within his own moved slightly, and her fingers tightened their hold upon his hand.

"Oh," said Gordon, indifferently, "it did not mean anything to him, you see, when he found he had lost her, and it could not mean anything to her. It is of no value. It means nothing to any one—except, perhaps, to me."

THE END.

Milton Keynes UK
Ingram Content Group UK Ltd.
UKHW030742071024
449371UK00006B/637